Narcissistic Family

Start your Road to Recovery from Narcissistic Abuse and Toxic Relationships with Parents Suffering from Narcissistic Personality Disorder

Lindsay Travis

Table of Contents

Introduction

Narcissistic personality disorder (NPD) is a disorder wherein the affected cannot control their emotions or urges to lash out. As this may sound like a borderline personality disorder, I assure you it is much different. Narcissists, as defined when we talk about someone who suffers with NPD, lack empathy and feeling for others as well as themselves. Any person who suffers with narcissistic personality disorder will manipulate, abuse, and take advantage of their victims. I would like to say they cannot help it, but like most people we all have the ability to think and in turn control our behaviors.

As a child we learn best from our parents and our peers no matter how supportive or unsupportive they are. If you have a parent who possesses narcissistic traits then you yourself may implement some of their traits in the future. All children like to be the center of attention and always try their best to impress their parents. A narcissistic parent comes in a few different forms. They might treat their child or children as a golden child." Another form of a narcissistic parent can manifest as them having their child serve their parents and do as they are told otherwise they get punished, manipulated, or belittled.

Narcissists, whether a part of your family or not, are abusive by nature and like to have complete control and power over you and everyone around them. They use holidays to their advantage and when they feel threatened, play the "blame game." This book explains the many forms of narcissistic abuse, answers the question of whether they can change, and provides you with much needed information to escape them. The sooner you can escape their wrath the better off you will be.

As narcissists can take control of you, they can also take away your self-esteem, self-worth, and have you second-guessing and questioning everything you do. The benefits you can experience by finally spreading your wings are endless. It is possible to hold true to yourself and love who you are as an individual. Now is the time to take back your control and reclaim the identity that your narcissistic parent has taken. Now is the time to break the cycle of their hoovering tactics and replace self-judgment with self-respect and self-control.

My promise to you by the end of this book, you will be able to define and identify the behaviors and abusive techniques of your narcissistic parent or sibling and release their power over you. My promise is that you will be able to gain a broader perspective and implement a healthy attitude into your life.

Are you ready to gain control and live a better more positive life? Are you ready to break free from their hold and learn who you are as an individual? Are you ready to commit to yourself and learn how to set boundaries and say no? Then you have come to the right place and by the time you are finished reading this book, you will have all your questions answered and be ready to live independently without the wrath of your insignificant family member.

Chapter 1: What is Narcissism?

Are you constantly looking over your shoulder, walking on eggshells, or second-guessing your every move when you think of a specific individual? Are you on edge all the time, questioning yourself, and feel like you are always messing up or in possible danger? When it comes to a certain person or people, do you feel like you never become heard, like your opinions don't matter, or that you get treated less than others when they are around? This is what it feels like to live with a narcissist in your life. The first step in beating a narcissist and moving forward with your life is to know what a narcissist is and what it really means when someone has narcissistic personality disorder.

So what is a narcissist? These people are part of what's called the dark triad – a group of people that fall under the personalities of a narcissist, psychopath, or sociopath. Each triad personality has their own unique differences and each of them is just as dangerous as the other. Some might say that narcissism is an act of self-love, but this is not at all the case. A narcissist is someone who has an idealized self-image that they feel as though they are grandiose compared to others. They hold themselves high on a pedestal not because they have high self-esteem but because they feel deeper feelings of self-insecurity, but deal with their insecurities by hurting others around them. You could say that narcissists are self-absorbed and they feel as though the world revolves around them. These types of people show patterns of being self-centered, arrogant, have a lack of empathy or feelings, and a need to be idolized or paid attention to by others. From the outside looking in at a narcissist, you may define them as cocky, selfish, manipulative, demanding, and judgmental.

While it's okay to be selfish or to think of yourself highly sometimes, the narcissists develop these attributes in every aspect and with everyone in their lives including personal relationships and business ones. Most of the time, someone with NPD doesn't realize that they are narcissistic and are happy with the way they live their lives due to the inability to feel empathetic. Because their world revolves around them, they don't feel the importance of anyone but themselves so they don't spend much time noticing or realizing the emotions of others. They spend their time blaming others for their actions and love to create or inflict emotional conflict without feeling shame or guilt around the events.

Depending on the type of narcissist, symptoms may vary. Some general signs and symptoms of narcissistic personality disorder may include the following:

- Implementing an exaggerated sense of self-importance

- Having the need for constant attention due to their sense of entitlement

- Expecting to be recognized for their achievements and if not recognized, lashing out

- Magnifying their achievements and talents

- Constantly obsessing over success, power, privilege, intelligence, beauty, etc.

- Gossiping about or belittling people they view as less than them

- Going out of their way to steal the light of people they view as better than them

- Taking people for granted to get ahead

- Being jealous of others, but still feeling as though people should envy them

- Coming off as boastful and arrogant

- Having an extreme need to have the best of everything, such as the best car, house, office, etc.

Narcissists have an extreme time being criticized and usually view people's advice as an attack or by feeling victimized. When this happens the narcissist is likely to become impatient or angry, become defensive and cruel, and have extreme mood swings due to their inability to regulate and control their feelings. Part of having NPD is that because of the lack of self-esteem and emotional regulation, they will react defensively to almost every situation if someone is not giving them what they want or telling them what they want to hear. They have a difficult time adapting to change and so they are in constant need of control. When things don't come through, conflict arises that seems like your fault and never theirs. People suffering with this type of personality disorder have hidden feelings of insecurity, shame, self-embarrassment, vulnerability, and humiliation.

There are many reasons why someone may have developed this disorder. Reasons can revolve around how they were raised, genetics, and chemical imbalances in the brain. It usually begins in early adolescence but it can show up in the early stages of child development as well. A household where neglect and different parenting styles exist may make a child growing up in that household vulnerable to their emotions and create subsequent confusion. In this sense, the narcissist is born. Some risk factors of an adult or teenager developing NPD are:

- Unhealthy relationships (whether experienced or witnessed)

- Excessive issues with work or school

- Depression, anxiety, and other mood disorders

- Chronic physical health problems

- Drug and alcohol abuse

- Suicidal tendencies

Someone experiencing the narcissistic personality disorder may not know that they have a problem even when continuous problems arise in their own lives. Since they are so quick to judge and blame others for their misfortunes, their views on the world is out of touch with what's right and wrong. These people are extremely sensitive to criticism of any sort (even positive) and likely misinterpret information due to their lack of empathy. Having a conversation with a narcissist will likely turn into disagreements, arguments, and from their lack of trust (trust issues) they don't see your point as valid because they think and believe what they want. If you are in a relationship with a narcissist such as being a friend, lover, parent, child, employer, etc. you may find yourself letting them 'win' arguments and give into their demands as it is easier not to argue and fight in order to avoid the rage and coldness of their words and actions.

Are You a Narcissist?

Personalities can get confusing, especially when you research and think to yourself that you might have some of these qualities in yourself. The thing about narcissists is that they can't help how they act. When they want something, they have to have it. If they want to change, that is when they will; but the change will only be on their terms when they will do something willingly. Sure you can be self-absorbed and high sprung. Maybe you have a difficult time controlling your own emotions and act out in rage—that doesn't mean you are a narcissist, but in the case where you are, you would most likely think and do the following:

1. Unilateral listening

If you were a true narcissist it wouldn't matter to you what other people think or say. What matters is your own opinion. When you listen, you listen to respond and don't actually hear what the other person is saying. You may not mean to do this, but this is automatic for you. If you find yourself responding to someone with a "but xxx" and talk about your own beliefs then you are undermining what the other person has said as if there was a physical backspace key in the form of words. So, if you only hear the thoughts and formations that pop up in your own head and feel as though you are right 100% of the time, then this could be a sign you may have NPD (Heitler, 2012).

2. It's all about you

Do you find yourself thinking these thoughts most of the time: *I am way more interesting than that person. My stories are better. You think that's bad, how about this. I am going to turn this conversation onto myself because it's about me,* or anything along those lines where you are constantly thinking about yourself? Perhaps you are waiting for an opportunity to bring the attention and focus onto yourself. Being in a conversation with a narcissist can feel like all the air is being hogged by them. You can't get a word in without them returning the conversation back to themselves because the hard truth is that they don't care what you have to say. Or maybe they do, but they find their own personal stories more important and feel like you should too. Do you find yourself going after what you want and putting your wants and needs ahead of others? Do you even use people to get to your destination without so much as a thank you or any sign of gratitude? This is another sign of narcissism.

3. You have special rules

Everyone has certain rules that we all need to follow like not cutting in line, no cheating on your partner, or not adding a zero to your taxes. These are hidden rules that most of society follows, but for a narcissist, these rules don't apply as they make up their own rules. If you feel superior to others and find yourself taking advantage of the 'rules' that are meant to be followed then consider yourself a narcissist.

4. You are very sensitive to criticism

Do you feel like people aren't actually giving you advice, but judging your every move or telling you how to live your life? Do you feel victimized when someone tells you about their feelings because you feel they are indirectly trying to hurt you? Narcissists feel objectified when someone tries to give them honest advice about the way they feel regardless of if they are trying to help or not. To a narcissist, criticism is a jab to them and they will jab back and worse because it's only about them and their feelings (Heitler, 2012).

5. You are never wrong

Imagine you apply for a job, have an interview, get rejected, and someone else takes your place. Do you go home and blame your spouse for not helping you get there? Have you ever felt like someone told you how they are feeling but you interpreted it as if they were blaming you instead of confiding in you? This is the way a narcissist thinks because it's impossible to accept they failed or made a mistake; it's impossible, as they can do no wrong. The reason they resist taking responsibility for their actions is because they have an 'all-or-nothing' way of thinking. If they do something bad then they must be bad and to be bad is not acceptable because they are superior. Narcissists don't make mistakes; they blame theirs on others who won't argue with them. They are conflict starters, and what better way to cause conflict?

6. Your actions are because someone made you do it

Ever done something you may have regretted but because you feel so much guilt and shame you pin your actions, based on your emotions, as happening *because of* someone else? For example, you get angry and the only reason you are angry is because someone said the wrong thing to you. Someone made you mad by doing what they did so that is why you behaved as you did. Narcissists do not have the ability to see their actions as their own doing because they think they wouldn't have done it if they weren't provoked or forced into it. So, by this logic, it must be the other person's fault (Heitler, 2012).

These signs don't automatically define you as being a narcissist but if two or more of them sound familiar, it may be beneficial to take a closer look into who you are. Start by seeing a psychologist or psychiatrist and let them know what's happening. If these signs of narcissism don't sound familiar but you think of someone else while reading them then you most likely have a narcissist in your life. The truth is you cannot tell a narcissist that they are suffering with the disorder because they wouldn't believe you anyways. A narcissist has to recognize and learn things on their own and in their own way. If they want to change they will, if not they won't. If you show clear signs of narcissism, the only way to beat it is to develop more skills such as decision-making skills, emotional understanding, and effective communication strategies. When you work on these skills you can reverse the narcissistic qualities and start building and working on a healthier you.

Narcissism in Children

When you think about it, all kids are naturally narcissistic due to their selfish behavior and their inability to understand other people's needs, desires, and feelings. Once a child reaches adolescence, they start to learn more independence and figure out how to think non-narcissistically. If a child does not get taught or learn healthy self-esteem, and confidence then they are bound to end up narcissistic stemming from their childhood environment and the attitudes or their parents and peers. A healthy level of self-esteem for a child is when they know that they are loved and worthy. They learn to know what they deserve and what they don't. When they become mistreated, they are more resilient which is what developing confidence and self-esteem is about.

Narcissists think of themselves and have deep hidden insecurities—like most young children. The difference between a child and a narcissist is that children learn to develop a sense of independence, which turns into high self-esteem, and they become a part of society. Whereas a narcissist is someone who never learns self-esteem and envies those who have it, so they go out of their way to disrupt and disturb others lives for their own personal growth. When the independence and self-centeredness doesn't change, the narcissist is born. A child will test buttons by whining, throwing temper-tantrums, and acting out as to see if they get what they wanted in the first place. A lot of the time, a parent will give into their child's wants so that the child will behave; however, doing this only teaches the child that they can walk all over people and get their way by acting inappropriately. This behavior will develop into adulthood while also giving them the notion that they are superior or grandiose compared to everyone else. If a child is upset and they don't get the "talking to" or the attention they need in these crucial moments, they don't get the opportunity to learn how to handle and develop their emotional intelligence skills. If this continues into adulthood, the narcissistic personality will dismiss others' feelings because they never learned how to manage their own.

As you can see, narcissism is bred into all of us starting at a very young age; but if a child is neglected, not taught the right skills to be a decent human being, or gets away with everything, they start to develop the worse traits of narcissism into adulthood. They are taught that using their emotions gets them what they want, pitting people against others gives them amusement, and striving for compliments by being selfish gives them a sense of power and control. A narcissist can be born under any circumstance where a child is neglected, or if they live in a household that is too strict, too lenient, or unstructured and unbalanced. Into adulthood, the narcissist–being raised as one– doesn't realize anything is wrong because their essential learning development has come and gone making them into who they are now. Once we are adults we behave and think based on the way were raised and had to grow up. That is why narcissism is so difficult to treat because it would be like shaping and changing an individual right from the root of the problem. Sometimes one's childhood could be great but people still grow to be narcissists because now they feel entitled to everything and always wanting more than what they have—unable to be grateful for anything they have now, and never being happy because of envy and low self-esteem.

So, what are the warning signs of a child or teenager becoming narcissistic?

- Constant use of narcissistic techniques such as bullying, threatening, blackmailing, belittling, and scapegoating people

- Competitive nature without the empathy of others' feelings when they lose (As long as their teen wins that's all that matters.)

- Constant exaggeration and lying to benefit themselves (When caught lying, it's everyone else's fault but their own.)

- Over-aggressive attitude when criticized or blamed for something

- Acting extraordinarily self-important and entitled

- Behaving as if attention is their right rather than being grateful to get it

- Expressing signs of being better than everyone (possibly stemming from their competitive nature)

- Unable to make, develop, and maintain friendships

- Arrogant and often rude by nature

These are most of the signs of how a narcissist will act and treat others–leaving out the manipulation tactics–as teenagers need to develop these beginning skills before they can fully understand manipulation (Johnson, 2017). If your child or someone else's starts to show one or more of these signs, the best thing you can do is teach the opposite of these tactics. Show them that being tough and dominant is not the way by nudging their behaviors towards kindness, gratitude, and honesty. Help your teen understand that in order to keep close relationships like friends, family, and intimate partners, it's better to think about their needs, wants, and feelings in front of your own. You can do this by role modeling effective communication skills. When you notice your child or teenager being temperamental or unbalanced with their mood, open up to them and offer some guidance. If they vent to you about making a mistake and how it is someone else's fault, make sure to build their self-esteem by telling them failure is part of life. Explain to them that blaming other people is wrong because no one causes us to do things that we did, as every decision we make is our own.

Parenting styles that develop a narcissistic child

Oftentimes particular types of parenting can birth a narcissist as briefly mentioned above. Other times, it can be because of the fact that the parents are also narcissists. Think of the "monkey see, monkey do" effect. All early aged children seek the attention and approval of their peers. So, the following scenarios are classic examples as to how children become narcissists through different parenting structures.

Scenario One – Narcissistic values

This type of parenting revolves around love being conditional when it comes to their child. Their 'motto' is go big or go home, if you can't be the best and beat the best why bother trying. With this frame of thinking, the parent will set too high of expectations for their child and only praise them when they have accomplished something exceedingly well. There is no room for mistakes and when mistakes are made the child is shown disapproval and harsh disappointment. This teaches the child that **love is conditional** as opposed to unconditional so the child will strive to do their best and feel rejected when they don't exceed their parent's expectations. Growing up this way teaches the child to continue this habit and to act in pure perfection otherwise they aren't good enough. Narcissists will use people to get ahead as a form of perfection, setting in motion a lifelong pattern and cycle of chasing success and power while mistaking success for true happiness.

Scenario Two – A narcissistic devaluing parent

This parent struggles with their own emotions and simply lashes out at their children for their inability to control their thoughts and feelings. Because the parent is irritable, angry, and holds unrealistically high expectations, the child suffers from the devaluing effect of it. If there is more than one child in the family, the parent will generally praise and keep one child elevated over the rest. Just as quickly as the 'good child' gets praised, they can just as easily become 'bad' and the parent moves onto the next child giving them the praise instead. It is never balanced between siblings because one child is always favored over the others—one at a time. In the case where only one of the parents is narcissistic, the non-narcissistic parent becomes devalued and criticized by the narcissistic parent when a disagreement arises leading to constant fighting and control battles. Growing up in this type of environment leaves a child feeling angry, humiliated, and insufficient or less than equal to others. This leads to low self-confidence and self-esteem levels. The outcome of this forms one of three types of child:

- **The defeated child:** Their self-esteem is diminished leading them to give up on trying so hard for approval and affection. This sets them up for depression and self-hatred, which leads to impulsive and addictive behaviors. The result is that they now believe they are worthless and will never achieve success because they were always devalued and told they had no potential.

- **The angry child:** Deeply engrained anger leads a child growing up to bully and devalue others that remind them of their parents. This leads to abusive toxicity in every relationship or *malignant narcissism*. This means that they not only feel as though they can succeed, but in their efforts, they will knock everyone down in the process.

- **The rebellious child:** This child takes on the opposite effects of the two and instead of believing what they have been told their whole lives instead chases acceptance by trying to prove themselves. They pursue greatness and success or whatever they want in every way that they can. In their best efforts, they try to avoid their inner-critic that their parents planted turning them towards a lifelong mission to get what they want if only to prove that inner-voice wrong (Greenberg, 2017).

Scenario Three – The golden child

Most narcissists enjoy the spotlight–so much so that they will do anything to take it from others and suck all the air out of the room by talking about themselves. In this scenario, the narcissistic parent avoids the spotlight themselves, but instead brags about their talented child. Even when the child is not very talented or has not done something remarkably well, the narcissist will over exaggerate the skills of their children. While this may not seem as too big of an issue, the child may develop some forms of narcissism due to the following reasons:

- If the child feels unrealistically viewed as more important (or less) then they feel as though their parents only value them *because* they are special, which contributes to an underlying insecurity problem.

- Due to the extreme praise, the child may belittle themselves when they see any type of flaw or imperfection leading to shame and insecurity.

- They won't exceed at other things because they are held so high on a pedestal that they feel they don't have to work at anything that they are not so good at. When they get constructive criticism later in life, they become oversensitive towards it and develop signs of narcissism.

Too much idealization from a parent can make a child have unrealistic views of themselves which leads them to believe flaws and imperfections are unacceptable. Perfectionism leads to insecurity, low self-esteem when mistakes are made, and the need to control everything. These attributes lead to narcissism very quickly.

Scenario Four – The exhibitionist's admirer

The exhibitionist parent only rewards their children if their child stays submissive to them. In this aspect, the child is fully taught and equipped with narcissistic values, because when they try to accomplish anything for themselves they get devalued by their parent. The child's sole role is to worship and serve their parent without ever trying to be equal or surpass the good qualities of their parent. Covert and closet narcissists are formed from being raised in this type of household because they are given the foundations of narcissism–attention and praise–for competing with the narcissistic parent and serving them. Also, they become devalued if they do anything other than what the narcissistic parent has asked or try to show extra achievements and act as someone who needs to be acknowledged as special. In short, the child only becomes accepted or valued as long as they support their egotistical exhibitionist parents.

In conclusion, a narcissist is born due to the environments and upbringing of their universe. As children instinctually have narcissistic traits at a young age, they aren't fully developed into NPD until later in life if they aren't taught how to act accordingly. Unstable and unhealthy upbringings—especially the lack of support and nourishment throughout life—can greatly improve the chances that a narcissist will be born and developed into a young adolescent from that childhood experience.

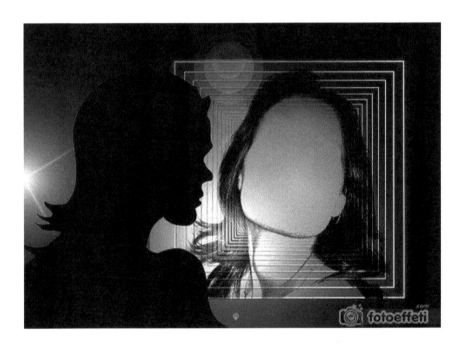

Chapter 2: The Abusive Narcissist

As you were learning, in the previous chapter, what a narcissist is and how they are born, you may have noticed that it starts in childhood but is raised up by the parent. Regardless of if the parent suffers from narcissistic personality disorder or not, children can still develop the disorder. A scenario where the parent treats their child as 'the golden child' is a perfect example of developing narcissism solely because they are feeding their own ego. While it may seem like a great idea to delve into all the interest and activities of your children's lives, in reality, you are actually taking more than you are giving because you are living *through* your child rather than living *for* your child. Another great example of the narcissistic parent is the scenario of the exhibitionist admirer because even though they support their child's interests, oftentimes their children's accomplishments are something they feel the need to compete with. Because of the fact that they don't want their children to overshadow them, they use their children's success to benefit and attract attention to themselves. All this does is take away their child's confidence and self-esteem because they are too busy saying: "That's my child, I raised that. Look at me go." All narcissistic parents will use their children's accomplishments to draw attention to themselves, which hurts and disregards the child's feelings. The reason for this is because the narcissist needs the spotlight in order to feel more advanced or worthy due to their own personal lack of self-esteem and empathy.

Aside from the fact that narcissistic parents fail to realize they are even doing this, they have their own additional reasons for why they do this to their children, regardless of the right and wrong of the situation. Some parents do it because of their own insecurities or need to boost their own self-confidence through their child's success. A healthy-minded parent will see their child as an individual with their own feelings, wants, and desires, while helping them achieve their goals and teaching healthy skills along the way. However, a narcissistic parent does not see their child as an individual and more like something they own due to the chemical imbalance of their brain structure, making them become selfish with their child's milestones. Another big reason that a parent will take the attention from their children is because someone with this disorder can confuse love with emotional hunger because their perception of love is distorted. While it may seem okay for the parent to shower their children with love, affection, and constant attention, the parent fails to understand that they are actually draining their child and keeping them from growing into the person they are destined to be. So what's the difference between love and emotional hunger? Love is an unconditional offering of encouragement, support, and attention. Whereas emotional hunger provides exactly the opposite, by instead of giving it to the child the parent is taking it. Which leads us to narcissistic abuse.

What Exactly is Narcissistic Abuse?

The struggle with knowing a narcissist is that anyone can be a narcissist and you won't actually realize it if you are about to get into a relationship with one until after you get to know them. The biggest problem about getting to know people and getting involved with relationships (friends, distant family members, or intimate) is that in our society, people tend to jump into relationships without fully getting to know someone first. So, down the road when things have finally become comfortable–if you are involved with a narcissist–they have already started to brainwash your mind so it becomes harder for you to leave and you become trapped. This is because a narcissist will use what's called the narcissistic cycle. In the beginning they use your weaknesses and flaws as leverage to get close to you and provide you with the support that you have been looking for. In this sense, your brain is now wired to view this narcissist as a person that gives you all your needs and wants so who cares if they belittle you, isolate you, and gaslight everything you do, right? Wrong. The thing about narcissists is they will take advantage of whatever they can the moment they meet you in order to get to know you. Then they can continue to use and diminish you while still seemingly giving you what you want and need through their charm and persuasion. This behavior is essentially manipulation. And as you may have guessed, this is also what narcissistic abuse is.

The three stages of a narcissistic abuse cycle

There are three parts to narcissistic abuse. They include: **idolization, devalue,** and **discard.** By understanding the cycle, you may begin to understand why a narcissist is incapable of having or developing a healthy relationship. In short, idolization means that someone will hold you high on a pedestal and tell you all of the things they know you want to hear. They will explain to you how you are so great and even go as far as showing it to you by taking you out on dates and showering you with affection. This is the charm stage where they are essentially winning you over. The devalue stage is when the narcissist has you under their wing, has already isolated you from your friends. They use this part of the process to knock down everything they have said to you or about you with no remorse. Oftentimes it's that they will compliment you but only on certain terms. For example, they might say "you look so amazing *when* you wear that," or "You are really great at what you do, *but* there is always room for improvement." The discard stage is when they leave you with nothing left. They have played their narcissism abuse tactics on you and you are left feeling less worthy, you have cut out your friends, and you now have to pick up the pieces because they couldn't care less about you. Then, just when you start to pick yourself up, they come back and the stages start again.

Here is a closer look at the three stages:

Idolization

The first stage is idolization where the narcissist will treat you like gold and shower you with attention. This stage may seem and feel good but behind the scenes, the narcissist is actually trying to get close to you to figure out your strengths and weaknesses as a person. It's the obsession stage where the narcissist confuses their feelings of infatuation with love, which eventually becomes obsession. They want to spend every minute with you, get to know you, talk about themselves mostly, and listen to only the dark parts about you so that they can exploit or magnify them later. This is where the codependent individual gets taken advantage of the most, because the truth is: a full independent person is someone the narcissist can never break down. While the narcissist feeds on and craves the attention and self-appraisal that they lack, the codependent will give the narcissist the supplies to fuel them. An example of this is that the narcissist will do everything in their power to be better than the last partner or person, whether they strive at being sexually better, more successful, richer, more attractive, etc. The codependent, while may actually be these things, would rather tell their spouse, or whoever the narcissist is, how amazing they are and expect little in return. So, in actuality the narcissist seeks people who are easy targets, ones that don't have a high self-esteem themselves, people that struggle with saying no, or ones that are 'working' on themselves but barely getting anywhere. They do this for the pure satisfaction of their own ego.

So how does the idolization stage work? Why is the narcissist so good at finding their victims? They find us because we have not established a true and pure love for and within ourselves. This is a problem for two reasons: one being that we are reliant on the love that someone else can provide for us so we never know what true love really is, if we don't first know and love ourselves first; two, the very fact that we have to rely on someone else to get love means that when it's gone, we get hooked to the person who gave it to us in the first place and try to win them back again and again to provide what we haven't learned to provide for ourselves. In this sense, the idolization stage is the drug that the narcissist provides us. Your payment to them is to give them attention and bow to their needs and wants while they give you the love and approval that you haven't given to yourself yet. The narcissist takes advantage of this factor which then creates an emotional high for both of you until something goes wrong, leading you to the devalue stage (Evans, 2017).

Devalue

As all relationships go wrong, deal with struggles and challenges, and have arguments that are essential to developing a healthy relationship, a narcissist will keep you inside their control as long as you still want the drug they provide. The devaluation stage is known as the red flag stage – but because the narcissist has you starry gazed, 'in love' and hooked, their abuse can be so minimal that it gets missed or you can easily create an excuse for the abuse. You might say: "h, they didn't mean it, they are so loving and supportive, everyone makes mistakes.' Yet the narcissist hasn't actually come out and apologized for anything, because they are still partially in the idolization stage. Instead of owning up to their mistake, they hide it by showering the victim with more love–an extra dose of the drug that the codependent is after. This continues to happen until the abuse becomes so extreme that there is no missing it, but now you are trapped and don't want to leave because you 'love' them. The devalue stage will manifest in the form of actions or words. Here are some examples of actions a narcissist might take during this stage:

- Dismiss your concerns or worries when you feel threatened or are in a dangerous situation

- Be unavailable when you are sick, stressed, or upset– oftentimes playing tit for tat when you need them the most

- Have a physical or sexual condition and not telling you about it, such as an STD or a heart disease (Evans, 2017).

There are more examples; however, the biggest warning signs are being dismissed or feeling 'off' or 'not right' after just being idolized and feeling special. When you feel like you can depend on them, but then get rejected or dismissed, these are clear signs of being with a narcissist. If the narcissist is smart enough to have you hooked, then the idolization stage is the first step in gaining your approval. Once they do this, they can devalue you, or dismiss you, as you will come up with justifications for their behaviors due to already experiencing the idolization stage. One thing to keep note of, is this: Healthy relationships have the ability for both partners to respect and care for each other and they will avoid treating each other in these ways. Another weapon in devaluing that the narcissist might use is verbal devaluing. These words can make someone feel self-doubt, confused, and make them more susceptible to the abuse (more dependent on the narcissist). Here are some examples of verbal weaponry that a narcissist will use:

- Insulting

- Gas lighting

- Threatening to leave

- Withholding information, attention, and intimacy

- Demanding needs like affection, compliments, and intimacy

- Blaming

- Accusing

This list of devaluing tactics of narcissistic abuse is not complete; however, if you feel as though you don't bow down to your partner or relationship, otherwise you could lose them, you are in the devaluing stage. One thing to keep in mind is that a healthy relationship will make you feel as though they are there for the long haul no matter what happens, always trying to make things better–not worse.

Discard

When the narcissist feels like they aren't getting what they need from the relationship anymore, they will unremorsefully discard you. If the attention you are providing them is not good enough, or undermines their image of themselves, you are no longer needed to them. This will results in a cold, disheartening break-up. In this case, the narcissist has taken your self-esteem, confidence, and whatever love you had for yourself away, forcing you to depend on them to get it; and just like that, they are done with you. But wait–they aren't quite done yet. They will show up at random points in your life to abuse you further, get inside your friends' heads, and turn your life even more upside down by being a constant reminder of what they gave to you and what you can never have again. Unless of course, you bow to them yet again. Any deep wounds from childhood creep back into the victim's life. Feelings of being abandoned and neglected resurface all over again; so the victim (you) will strive to be a part of their lives again. But what you are actually doing is giving into their superiority by wanting to stay; in which case, they will stay gone, because now they are getting your attention in a different way. You might be thinking it will get better if you just bow down to them again, but they will use your past arguments and any failures in the relationship against you as a reminder not to do it again, leaving you feeling helpless and unhappy and them feeling on top once again. A true healthy relationship is supposed to end on good terms and never to be confronted again in such unfriendly manners (Evans, 2017).

Narcissistic Abuse Tactics

The cycle of narcissistic abuse will draw you in, make you want them more, and then leave you feeling emptier than before. There are many ways a narcissist will do this. It's essential to learn about the techniques so that you can notice them and deal with them BEFORE getting involved. Although all abusive partners or relations may use some of these methods, the difference between a narcissist and a potentially healthy partner is that the narcissist will use these following techniques excessively at every chance they get. They do these because of the inability to take responsibility and feel empathy.

1. Gas lighting

Gas lighting is when the offender will say: "that didn't happen;" "you are imagining things;" or "are you sure you're not going crazy?" The purpose of gas lighting is to make you question yourself and if they succeed, they can now use any accusation you make as a form of distorting your reality. They have now convinced you that you were imagining things. Gas lighting controls trust and when you lack trust in yourself, you start doubting everything around you, which leads to low self-confidence.

2. Projection

Narcissists hate admitting to their faults and over time they will have developed a sense of emptiness and insecurity. Projection is where someone will accuse you of something they actually have or feel inside themselves. For example, if the narcissist feels as though they are incompetent or if they have lied about something, they will point the blame or lash out at their partners for lying or being incompetent. They may call you needy or clingy in their own attempts to not be needy and clingy; but knowing that they are, they instead force you to believe that you are.

3. Nonsensical conversation

Arguing with a narcissist is pointless because rather than focusing on the point, the narcissist will throw you off track of your main thought by gas lighting, projecting, blaming, and insulting you if you decide to call them on their stuff. To them, your thoughts don't matter and while they spend enough time beating themselves up about their faults, they don't take your criticism about their shortcomings very well. For example, you may have disagreed with them about the sky being red and now out of nowhere your childhood, family, friends, and everything you thought you knew gets questioned because of your own opinion regardless as to how irrelevant it is to the point.

4. Over-generalizations

Narcissists do not take the time to consider your criticism or look at something in a different perspective; instead, they would rather generalize everything you say into one thing. They don't take into account what was originally stated but rather they label you and dismiss your perspective altogether. For example, the abuser might say: "You are too sensitive or never satisfied." This way, they now have you thinking about defending yourself rather than on the actual problem of them coming home late, or picking up after themselves, or whatever the case may be

5. Nitpicking or excessive nagging

Do you have a successful career? Do you have your license and a good car? Why haven't you started that project yet? Did you even want to get your hair done? This is the narcissist's way of pointing out small details of all of the things you haven't accomplished or aren't doing yet. Rather than supporting your success, they help you focus on what you haven't achieved yet as a way to keep you from ever achieving it. Even when you have accomplished it, they wouldn't notice because of their sole recognition of themselves. So when you do get that haircut you wanted, they may say something like: "Where's mine? All you do is think of yourself." If you argue that they didn't ask or didn't want to come, they will then us the tit for tat or blame game about what you did to them to justify why they didn't come, ultimately avoiding the original problem from the beginning.

6. Destructive conditioning

Destructive conditioning is where the narcissist will use what they once valued about you and put you down or take back what they said by saying: "I thought that way because of xxx or because you did xxx." When holidays come around, they have already isolated you and turned the people against you in such a way that your goals and celebrations have become ruined by this new image of what you can and cannot accomplish. They do this because they prefer your attention to be more focused on them rather than on yourself or your family and other friends.

7. Control

The easiest way for a narcissist to get control over you when they can't control you is to control how others see you. They start playing the victim card and make you out to be the bad guy to slander your name and ruin your reputation. This is so when they leave you (discard stage), you have no one to support you or fall back on except for them.

8. Bait and create innocence

A narcissist will seem innocent but bait you into coming back to them or into a mindless argument as to gain a sense of entitlement or superiority. For example, a narcissistic ex may still have some of your things at their house. While they never allow you to go over and get it, out of boredom one day they might randomly text. They might even make it seem as if they are someone else (their new partner) in order to lure you in. You having some stuff still there may feel obliged to go over and grab your stuff only to be bombarded by them alone (when there was no other person there to begin with). They now have an excuse that you went to their property unannounced. This is one example of baiting and creating innocence. It helps to understand and realize when you are being baited so that you can withdraw from the situation and not engage in their mindless activity (Arabi, 2019).

There are tons of tactics a narcissist will use to get you trapped or to stay with them. It makes it more difficult for you because along with these manipulative tactics, they continue giving little glimpses of hope—little hints or moments reminding you that a normal person is still in there. They do this so that you will continue to justify their behavior and fall deeper for them. They can keep you being useful to them and under their control.

Why Are Narcissists Abusive?

Narcissists struggle with maintaining control over their emotions. They do not have high emotional intelligence, and they struggle with being sociable people because of their excessive lack of self-esteem. Most people have self-esteem issues, but combined with internal insecurity, a childhood of abandonment or over-praise, and the inability to be empathetic, it is a recipe for narcissism disorder. So, in this sense it may be safe to say that the narcissist doesn't know better or maybe they just don't want to work on themselves to be better people. Regardless of their own personal reasons, narcissists continue to be abusive because they have gotten away with it their whole lives and don't really know how to be any way other than narcissistic. Some reasons why are as follows:

1. They have conditional self-worth

When a narcissist thinks of their self-worth, they think "I feel good about myself *if* I feel better than you *if* you agree with me/ *if* you tell me how amazing I am." The conditional self-worth is why they bully others to make themselves feel better or build themselves up. They crave the attention but also compare their strengths and weaknesses to others around them. If they see someone else as better than them, they will bully these people as a way to make themselves feel more important.

2. They need validation

Along with the conditional self-worth feeling, the narcissist needs to be validated for all their hard work. Meaning they need to be noticed by someone without them being told in order to feel good. Once they are acknowledged for their efforts, they strive for more and more because it is never enough to have just one person's opinion of them, they need others to notice that they are the best so they can feel like the best and to become the best.

3.Their motivation stems from fear

They experience fear both internally and externally in how they interpret what you do or will do, and then how they will react to it. Their main fear is that they are not good enough, not unlovable, and unworthy of not just themselves but to other people. Because this is a deep-rooted problem, the narcissist is not entirely aware of it and they act upon their fear by constantly chasing the love. When they don't receive it, they abuse.

4.Anger is the forefront emotion

A narcissist will feel angry over feeling vulnerable because they do not want to show their weaknesses to others. This also associated with their feelings of self-worth. Anger has become automatic to them because they are trying to protect themselves from weakness.

5.Their behavior has nothing to do with you

It's best to take whatever a narcissist says with a grain of salt because one moment they can take what you say as a joke, and the next time you say something they can blow up with rage. Their ego is what propels their actions so if they have a strong dose of coddling of their ego, they will be more kind. So if their ego is dampened or altered in any way they can feel great stress and cause all types of conflict.

The only thing to do when it comes to narcissistic abuse is to notice a narcissist, and look the other way. Their love is fabricated, their self-image is disproportioned, and their perception of you and the world is to serve them. Only the narcissist can truly find pure potential and self-growth by recognizing and accepting who they are. They must then seek professional advice for themselves and take part in some personal growth classes. However, if the narcissist doesn't want to change, they won't. Oftentimes they don't like hard work because they are too busy putting their 'dirty laundry' onto others. Escape the narcissist by learning about them, learning how to spot them in the first five minutes, and ignore their hovering techniques by being aware of and honest with yourself. In order to fully move on from the overpowering abuse they put you through you must to respect yourself, set boundaries, and love who you are today without expecting anything more or less.

Chapter 3: The Escape Plan

In the previous chapter you learned all about the many ways a narcissist will abuse in order to get under your skin and push you to unhealthy mental limits. You also learned that narcissists may or may not know better and for them to make things right, or even positive for themselves, they must first acknowledge they have a problem and *want* to change it. Without these two ingredients of the recipe for getting better, a narcissist will stay a narcissist. They will continue to abuse and pick out the 'weakest' links to use as their victims in the manipulation game they call life. So what if they don't want to change? Or, what if they don't realize they are the problem to begin with? That's where you need to come up with an escape plan. Even if the narcissist *is* willing to change, an escape plan is always the best route, not only for yourself but for them as well as it teaches them boundaries and gives them the opportunity to realize that change needs to happen before getting involved with you again. By having an escape plan in place you teach yourself self-respect and create healthy boundaries so that you don't fall into a narcissist's trap again. Although escaping the narcissist has many benefits, actually following through and learning not to fall into the same trap again is going to be the hardest part. Narcissistic abuse is potentially one of the hardest relationships to recover from because they have implemented deep-rooted problems within your mind that you now have to overcome.

First, I would like to mention just a few reasons why someone may stay in an abusive relationship before diving right into the escape plan of leaving the narcissist. People stay in abusive relationships for many reasons, including being fearful of what their abuser will do if they leave. Some people may fear that the secrets and vulnerability they presented to their friends, lover, or otherwise will be outed to the world if they try to leave. Sometimes, a victim may stay simply because they mistake the abuse as love. If the victim has never been in or witnessed a healthy relationship this abusive relationship feels normal to them. These are just some reasons someone will stay longer than they should with a 'normal' abuser. Escaping a narcissist may feel close to impossible for other reasons. They include but are not limited to the previous reasons. Here are a just a few short examples of why someone might stay in an abusive narcissistic relationship:

- **Love bombing:** The victim (you) will stay because the abuser (the narcissist) will show little doses of love and affection here and there. The love that they give you is the drug you can't stay away from (as explained in the previous chapter) because you cannot tell the difference between emotional hunger and true, healthy love.

- **You are an empath:** People who are empathetic will have too many feelings or sympathy for people who play the 'victim' card and show effort here and there. It's the abuser's goal to show you they can change, but then never will never actually have a goal in mind. Empaths will try to fix the pain deep rooted in the abuser, while the narcissist will anticipate the attention because the empath worships them. Thus they never change.

- **Trauma bonding:** Trauma bonding is when the abuser will do this 'back and forth' thing (I love you, I don't love you; I'm sorry, I am not sorry) to hook you and give you false hope that they really are sorry and they really do want to try. Eventually things always end up the same. It's like the narcissist is playing cat and mouse with you, keeping you on the line and feeding you love and affection as long as you continue to do what they want. Thus leaving you with the high you felt in the beginning.

- **Downplaying the abuse:** Due to the narcissists smart manipulation tactic of gas lighting, the abuser will continue to distort one's reality and keep the victim exactly where they want the victim to be. You (the victim) may notice a 'change' for about three weeks until you start being vulnerable again and opening up or letting your guard down, then BAM! The narcissist will abuse again. But they downplay their abuse because they were 'so good' for three weeks, and "they didn't mean to."

- **Repetition compulsion:** This is something that happens automatically if you have been abused before or witnessed unhealthy relationships in your past. While someone tries to stay away from abusive relationships, they end up falling into them again because of the fact they are trying so hard to avoid it. When abuse is deep-rooted into someone's brain, they don't know how to tell the difference between healthy and unhealthy because unhealthy is all they know. The problem is because the victim will always try to fix their abusive partner if they see they are damaged by saying to themselves: *"Things will be different this time because I can do xxx or I can try xxx. They are not my ex, so I can give them a shot." To* their demise, things always end up the same–unhealthy and uncontrollable.

Understanding why you cannot leave is one thing, but really understanding yourself is the only way you can truly escape a narcissist and not fall into the same trap again. A lot of people have triggers as to what they see as attractive and enticing. But these people usually fall into abusive relationships (narcissistic or otherwise) because they have not learned how to truly give to themselves what they look for other people to give to them. This is so important to understand in the moving on and moving forward process of escaping a narcissist.

Leaving the Narcissist

The very first step in leaving a narcissist for good is to be completely sure you want to. You must be 100% sure, because any doubt in your mind about leaving them will have you returning back to them again. If this happens things will continue to repeat in the cycle of idolize, devalue, and discard. Furthermore, say you are finally done; you are fed up with the mental exhaustion, emotional confusion, and the constant effort of trying but getting nowhere. Now you are just unsure with what to do next—or first, for that matter. The following steps are sure to get you started and on to your next step of reclaiming your life again. Keep in mind that before you start the escape plan, you must let go of all fear and be okay with completely falling apart and feeling empty for the first little while. I promise you, it will all feel worth it in the end. You must find the motivation to continue moving forward and not give into your critical mind, which expresses itself through the thoughts that cause you to go backwards instead of forwards. So let's take a look:

1.Start by cutting all contact

No contact means absolutely any contact. Block their cell number, their social media profiles, setup rules on your email inboxes to make sure you cannot receive emails from them, etc. By doing this, you will not be notified when they try to reach out to you, which then cuts off their control and power over you.

2.Don't linger on the goodbye

It's usually best to break up in person but in the case of breaking it off with a narcissist, it may be wise to break it off using a text message. Be clear in your message and state the simple reasons why. If you choose to do it in person, it will be easier for them to suck you back in using one of their many famous 'hoovering' techniques. Hoovering will be explained later in this chapter. Once the text is sent, immediately block them so that they cannot respond and draw you back in. In short, hovering is a technique they will use to draw you back to them by telling you everything you have been wanting to hear from them, but once you are back with them (or change your mind), things go back to as they were and potentially even worse.

3.Block ties and associations

One hoover technique is to contact you through your mutual and even non-mutual friends. Even worse, you may have friends that the narcissist got into the heads of and so those friends or family members will convince you to go back. They may start by being unsupportive with the breakup then try to get you two back together because 'you were so good together.' Most of the time despite your family or friends best intentions, they never see what goes on behind the scenes. When you try to explain, they don't believe you because they now feel closer with your abuser than they do to you. Get as far away from the narcissist as possible and if that means blocking certain people associated with them, then that's what you must do. It's a crucial step in regaining your mental well-being.

4.Create a journal as to why you left

When everything is officially over–said and done–your mind may play tricks on you and reminisce on all the good things and good memories that you went through with them. In this sense, your mind will be trying to convince you that things weren't so bad. You must challenge these thoughts and write down all of the reasons why you left in the first place–the sooner the better, so that the memories are fresh in your mind. You can do this before you break it off or after. Better yet, when the abuse starts, keep a journal of your experience. This way when you finally end things for good, you have something to look back on as a reminder not to go through it again. Write down what happened, how you felt, and where you were before meeting them as opposed to where you are after meeting them. Put in as much detail as you can so that there is no way your mind can convince you to go back.

5.Assume the narcissist doesn't care (because they don't)

Narcissists are raised and have deep rooted self-esteem issues (learned in Chapter One). They don't mean to abuse you, but they do it because of their issues to build themselves up (learned in Chapter Two). What you need to learn and understand now for the escape process is that the narcissist is only looking for power and control. You were only a target for them as their definition of love is distorted and altered based on their own personal experiences. Think of your relationship as a business deal–that's all it ever was. You gave them the attention they craved and needed while they gave you the temporary high of 'love' based on your need for it and your emotional hunger. The relationship was actually only a dose-distorted reality that you convinced yourself that you needed. When the narcissist feels like something is over, it won't take them long to move on to their next victim so keep this in mind when you are in the midst of your escape. Also, don't take it personally, as this is the only way the narcissist knows how to live their lives–unless they get the professional help they require.

6.Grieve

Every relationship–healthy or not–needs a grieving process. It doesn't matter if they have moved on or if they are still strung up on you (only because they are seeking ways to gain power over you again). Ending a relationship is like finding out that you have lost a loved one. Give yourself time to grieve the relationship because this step is crucial for not falling into another narcissistic relationship. During your grieving process you are most vulnerable to taking them back, but keep a note of the fact that the narcissist got to know your strengths, weaknesses, and vulnerabilities in the beginning so that they could literally be the person you needed at this time. They are master manipulators and will do it again if you give them the chance. Recognize how you feel now as opposed to how you felt before your relationship with the narcissist. Maybe you were happier, maybe you had everything going for you, maybe you were richer, or maybe you were more balanced. Part of the grieving process is to recognize where you were, what went wrong, and why you left. Sadness, shock, disappointment, and frustration are all part of the process to moving on and grieving your relationship. Sit with each of these feelings until you manage to control each one on a healthy level.

7.Stay busy and distracted

Sitting with your emotions learning to feel each and every single one can be healthy for you, but if you give them too much attention, it can also be very bad. When you feel sadness or are confronted with a memory that reminds you of the 'good' times, allow yourself to smile or cry about it, and then quickly redirect your attention. Some ideas for creating a healthy distraction are to: create a daily exercise routine, practice self-love and self-respect exercises, meditate, learn something new, do something new, etc. Every distraction technique should be something that furthers personal growth because learning and growing is what it truly means to escape the narcissist. Find something that makes you happy and do it.

Part of escaping a narcissist is to learn more about yourself and set healthy boundaries. Use the breakup as a chance to find yourself and love yourself. Take the spare time and emotional freedom to your advantage as a means to work on yourself and your potential. This process involves being positive and learning how to challenge your inner-critic, which is the voice inside your head that tells you: *you can't*. When you believe that you *can*, you will soar. Fearing the unknown and making mistakes are the fundamentals to success and happiness because fear can either hold you back or help you gain a different perspective. Making mistakes shows you that you are not perfect and helps you create and make wiser decisions in the future. Perhaps the biggest thing that will help you in this moment is becoming more aware of yourself by learning what you truly want, need, and desire and figuring out how to provide that for yourself.

What is Hoovering?

Hoovering is a technique a narcissist will use to get you back. Usually it's when they are struggling to find their next victim and their lack of self-love becomes unbearable, so they will literally do anything to get you back to get their dose of 'love.' It is important to take a mental note while reading about these techniques that although most of them are used by a narcissist, some ended relationships will attempt to use the same techniques. However, not everyone is a narcissist because they do the same thing, use the same tactics, or have some characteristics in common. The biggest difference you will find in a narcissist when they use these hoovering methods is that when one doesn't work they will often move onto something else to see if that one will work. A healthy respectable relationship won't continue to try after realizing that it is over; however, they may just be craving closure if they haven't got it yet.

Some important things to know about the hoovering method are that there are multiple ways to draw someone back in but when a narcissist does it, it's usually after a long period of silence (also a technique to keep you wondering about them). Most hoovering techniques start off as discreet, but become noticeable when their efforts fail or when you don't give into them. For example, if the narcissist randomly shows up at a place you are going to be and makes conversation with you about how you have been and you engage with them; you are already hooked. Next, you will be laughing together and they will be the person you fell for all over again. This is their foot in the door back into your life because even though it may seem like it stops there, the silence will return and you will have moved backwards in your escape process by thinking about them and wondering what could be. The tricky thing about the hoover method is that the narcissist already knows what makes you tick. They have defined what makes you happy because they created that world for you. In this reality, they know how to make you come back even when you never thought you would. Here are some quick examples of the hoovering methods that will be used:

Promise of closure

- "I have something to tell you, it's really important."

- "I forgot to mention something to you that has to do with your future."

- "If you don't believe me, you can ask me anything and I will be honest with you."

Does this sound familiar? This is a hoovering technique that piques your interest and has you fall for whatever their information is. They promise you closure and somehow convince you that it's important to meet with them right away so that you can end things properly. While they may seem genuine, you take a chance and go just to be let down because it was the exact opposite of closure.

Just one more night

- "I miss having you here, maybe one more night with me for old time's sake will help us both move forward; if that's what you really want."

- "Can we please just pretend everything is okay because I really just need one more night? Don't you miss me?"

Your mind is now flooded with memories of being together, those passionate nights that drew you together, and the calling of your affection just wanting to be close to them again. Whether it is sexual with an intimate partner, or happiness and traditions with a close family member or friend, the narcissist is calling on your weaknesses. Don't do it.

Speaking your love language

Love languages are someone's language of love through gifts, physical touch, words of affirmation, acts of service, and quality time. The narcissist will,

- Send you a gift with a special note that only you can interpret.

- Give you a box of your stuff with a few added things that remind you of them and your time together.

- Reach out to you through music.

It's best to ignore all their efforts or get a supportive friend to delete the music, destroy the notes, and give your box to charity or get rid of it. It may be difficult for you to do this, but that's where your journal of why you left comes in handy so that you can remind yourself why you are doing this. Remembering that this is only a hoover method should keep you on track.

False accusations

- "I heard you were on a dating app, thanks a lot I guess I meant nothing to you."

- "I know you are already dating someone else, guess you really are selfish and never loved me."

- "I can't believe you are hanging out with MY friend, how dare you."

Even if you are not doing these things, the narcissist will come up with creative ways to accuse you of something just to get a reaction or a response out of you. It's their way of getting attention from you and the recognition that you still care. If they know that you care, then they know they can easily get to you. When they can get to you, they can abuse you. Remember this and don't give in.

Remembering important dates

- "Wishing you all the best at your interview."

- "Today was supposed to be our anniversary / friendaversary/ family get together, I had so many plans for us. Wishing you the best though."

- "How did your meeting with the doctor go?"

The narcissist will show you that they care or give you false hope that they ever did care by remembering dates that were important to you. It's a method to get you to rethink your break up as a means to make you think that they actually do care about you. Remembering the pain and struggle they put you through should be the first response you think about–NOT about how you are going to respond to their messages.

I am here if you need someone

- "I am here for you always as friends when you need me."

- "I wish we never got into a relationship because our friendship meant so much more to me than what we ended up being."

- "If you need help moving, babysitting, or hosting your upcoming party, let me know. I am more than available to you."

Since the narcissist had you isolated, they know that you are struggling for support. For all you know they could still be in contact with some of your closest friends, filling their heads with lies. They might be giving them reasons as to why you two don't talk anymore—despite you not doing anything wrong. They are trying to play on your heartstrings by giving you what you crave— someone familiar and 'comfortable' to talk to.

Threats of an emergency or self-harm

- "I really need you, I am in the hospital and don't trust anyone else to be with me but you."

- "I fell down my stairs and need you to take me to the hospital or come over immediately. I know you will if you still care."

- "If you don't come to me, I will be forced to do something horrible to myself."

When you give into these calls, you are showing them that you are still there for them thus leading them to believe there is still hope for you guys. In reality, they are playing on your empathetic nature to see how far they can go. If you believe that they honestly need help, tell someone you trust or respond by giving them a hotline number for someone they can talk to. Most of the time, someone will not actually hurt themselves. Often they would want to hide it and not say anything to anyone due to the embarrassment of it. A narcissist will not be this vulnerable to you.

Bad feeling

- "Did something bad happen to you? I got this overwhelming anxious feeling that something did."

- "I had a nightmare that something was terribly wrong, are you okay?"

This method is used to make you believe that they care or that they ever did. The truth is that they are very good in understanding who you are, and what a normal person (without the disorder) would do. So they will try to reach out to you by acting like a caring friend or by doing what a supportive person would do. Giving into this would only prove to them that you haven't unblocked them and you still think about them.

In short, hoover means that your abuser uses unfair tricks to win you over. They show that they care–like you wanted the whole time–or they show that they have taken time to think about why you ended things in the first place. The main difference between someone using hoovering techniques and someone who genuinely cares about your well-being, is that a healthy relationship will respect your wishes and support your decisions. If you are ending the relationship because of narcissistic abuse and the traits you endured then these methods should be a clear sign that they only want to win you back to abuse you again. Keep this in mind before responding to any of these attempts. If you are really questioning their intentions or wondering if change has really happened, test your theory by not responding and pay attention to the outcome of it. If they become angry or more aggressive, then you know it's a hoovering technique to put you through unhealthy mental frustration again.

Chapter 4: Can a Narcissist Family Change?

The thing about narcissism is that every human being on this earth has some narcissistic quality in them. If you think about it, we all want to feel special, we all want the spotlight (in some circumstances), and we are all selfish in our own ways. Basically we are all trying to stand out and make a difference that will impact the world in some way. So the fact of the matter is that narcissism is NOT a disorder. It only becomes a disorder when our personality of narcissism exists in all aspects of our lives. It's only when we don't understand how to manage our emotions along with a lack of empathy that narcissism becomes a personality disorder. Looking at narcissism in this way is like looking at anyone with a personality disorder such as borderline personality disorder, or a mood disorder like anxiety and depression. Can these be managed, helped, cured, or even changed? Yes, however, it takes a great deal of work, commitment, patience, and desire to actually want to follow the advice of professionals to get better and manage narcissism traits. Just like for anxiety, in order to get better you must change different aspects of your life to manage and cope with it such as diet, the way you think, the way you worry, the way you basically live life. Prescription medication will only cover the problem but if you really want a fulfilling life, you must put into the work to overcome it just like any mental health or physical health problem.

For narcissists to truly change they have to be comfortable with getting to know themselves on a deeper emotional level so that they can uncover the underlying shame and insecurities they have. They need to learn how to make internal sacrifices such as giving up the spotlight, being more aware of their actions so that they can put someone else first, and asking for help when they feel too ashamed to do so. In order to get a narcissist to *want* to change, they must be faced with three things:

Leverage

To get the narcissist looking for therapy or even consider therapy, there must be leverage of some sort. This could involve the fear of losing someone close to them, the threat of losing their job or power, or their social status and reputation must be at risk.

A therapeutic approach

Just as cognitive behavioral therapy **(CBT)** could work for anxiety sufferers, or dialectical behavior therapy (**DBT**), for people with borderline personality disorder, narcissists need to find the right corrective therapy that works. A therapy such as schema therapy may work for narcissists as this focuses below the intellectual and reexamines the emotional narrative in the brain.

A good therapist

A good therapist is someone who does not become attached or become persuaded easily. The perfect therapist for the narcissist is one who doesn't trigger the narcissist and who can set strong boundaries. This would consist of the therapist putting themselves in a mindset of 'parenting' the vulnerable part of the narcissists mind while also keeping them accountable for their thoughts and actions. When the 'perfect' psychologist is found, they will teach the narcissist how to change. The change will look like this:

- Teaching them the ability to understand their actions and how their actions create negative emotions and thoughts (or vice versa)

- Teaching the narcissist the consequences of what can happen due to these uncontrollable thoughts and feelings, which in turn gets them taking responsibility for ALL of their actions

- Allowing the narcissist to believe that they have choices and based on their choices they define their outcome (tackling the abusive behavior)

- In the midst of anger, sadness, loneliness, etc. is able to teach the narcissist to be aware of their choices as to why they are upset and then how to make different choices apart from how they feel

As you can see, the process of helping a narcissist to change can be quite a big deal. Still, if a narcissist is in denial about there being a problem then they will be unable to admit their faults and would prefer to continue down the path they are going. The problem with this is that it can be dangerous to argue and fight with a narcissist, as it can be extremely difficult for the individual who suffers because they don't understand why they do what they do. If you come right out and tell them they are narcissists, their extreme sensitivity to criticism could damage you more than your criticism damages their ego (How to Deal with a Narcisisst, 2018).

A Family of Narcissists

When we talk about narcissism in the family, we aren't just talking about one narcissist. Narcissistic tendencies or characteristics can affect the entire family, because if you are a narcissistic parent, then you are bound to raise your child narcissistically. If you have a narcissistic child, there is bound to be someone in the family making excuses for it, which only makes the child more susceptible to maintaining their traits. This can greatly affect every holiday spent together, making on afternoon with your family members a catastrophe to remember. Here is what I mean when I say narcissism affects the whole family.

- **The Enabler:** This includes the spouse of a narcissist, the grandmother of a narcissistic child, or a close sibling.

The enabler enables the narcissist's behavior by justifying their actions to avoid further conflict.

- **The Flying Monkey:** These family members can include anyone and is typically described as someone who abuses the other members on behalf of the narcissist. For example, an adult sister may have cut contact with the narcissistic sibling and if the parent is the flying monkey they may make the sister feel shame and guilt for cutting those ties.

- **The Scapegoat:** This family member is the bold member who calls the narcissistic person like they are–a person with NPD. They would rather call it like it is instead of lavishing the narcissist with praise and attention. Usually this type of behavior results in the rest of the family getting upset with the scapegoat due to their unsupportive attitude towards the narcissist.

- **The Golden Child:** Usually this is a child of a narcissistic parent, who gets treated with more praise and attention than everyone else. This creates conflict with other family members, as the golden child can be used to scapegoat or gaslight other members within the family. Oftentimes, the position of the golden child can be shifted when they disagree or withdraw from the idolized view of their parent, as the parent will then become abusive and gaslight their own child (How to Deal with a Narcissist, 2018).

These family attributes can make for messy holidays and may take time for the family together as a team to change. Although, it's a big ordeal for just one narcissist to change, in order to get the whole family on board and willing to change there would need to be certain therapeutic properties in place with a set structure of how things will pan out. Not only that, it must work for everyone, otherwise the whole thing could fall apart and the traits of narcissism only worsening.

Narcissistic Holidays

There are two things that can happen on family holidays, either the narcissist in the family doesn't show up, or they do and the get-together becomes tense. Holidays such as Christmas, birthdays, Thanksgiving, New Year's, etc. can trigger a narcissist's rage and perfectionist tantrums. Trying to enjoy the holidays does not just consist of or affect the narcissist himself, but the victims as well, especially when the narcissist has succeeded in isolating their victim. If you just ended a relationship or stopped contacting the narcissist, there can be an empty void during the holidays especially if your personality revolved around them e.g., doing things for them to avoid their wrath, guilt-trips, and blame games. Perhaps the most challenging part of moving forward with your life is trying to refigure out who you are due to the overwhelming freedom from making constant sacrifices and serving your narcissist.

Holidays, however, are perfect for getting back on track (if the narcissist isn't present). They allow you to open up with your family again, eat healthy, and rebuild relationships with supportive, positive people that you once had a lot of. Aside from rebuilding relationships, make sure in these special holidays ahead that you also care for yourself. Think of your care as how you would take care of your children if they were lovesick or otherwise. Exercise, sleep well, drink water, give yourself love, tell yourself positive things that build confidence, etc. There are other things you can do this holiday season to boost yourself up after a narcissistic injury including:

1. Be patient with yourself

You can't expect to move on right away and you can't expect yourself to feel happy immediately either. You may feel relieved until the memories of you together remind you of the joy you felt with them during the holidays. Do what makes you happy while remembering that nothing has to be completely perfect and it doesn't have to be a complete disaster either. If this year, you don't feel like enduring the festivities, then give yourself more time because you don't have to do anything you don't want to.

2. Embrace what was gone that you can rebuild

What traditions did you used to celebrate before the narcissist came into your life? Was it looking at Christmas lights? Was it getting dressed up for Halloween? Was it giving thanks by helping out someone in need? Whatever it was, you should continue doing them because the narcissist hasn't ruined these yet. If you don't pursue what you used to do, then only you are the reason they ended.

3. Recognize toxic people and avoid them

Become familiar with toxic people and people who are unsupportive in your adventures because having them around is only going to slow your recovery process down. Go through all your friends, family members, and relationships to figure out who is here for you and who is not. Which people want the best for you and which only use you to get what they want. The toxic people in your life need to be avoided (if you can) and the non-toxic should be sought out to spend more time with.

4. Give, give, give

It's a proven fact that when we give to others, the endorphin hormones get released which is the 'feel good' hormone in our brains. Giving to other people by donating, helping someone unload their groceries, or simply just giving someone a piece of advice are all ways that you can give to others while feeling good about yourself. Other ideas involve cleaning litter off the streets, planting trees, or volunteering at a shelter for animals or people.

It can be difficult to enjoy the holidays when the narcissist isn't around because they are familiar. As soon as you start practicing to be with yourself and loving yourself, the days ahead will get better and eventually you will laugh at yourself for holding your breath for the abuser. Enjoy the absence of their added baggage and stress, and remember to stay compassionate to yourself and others.

Narcissists LOVE holidays, particularly because it is easier to steal the light and show their ego off as to be better or more perfect than everyone else. They like control, conflict, and attention. What better way to be prideful and boastful during the holiday season? I've discussed how holidays can go on without the narcissist, but what if the narcissist is still present during a holiday? Here is what a holiday might look like with a narcissist included in the family get-togethers.

The curator's touch

From the immaculate tree on Christmas to the fully decorated yard on Halloween, to the best fireworks on New Year's, holidays give the narcissist a chance to show off and compete with everyone around them. If you are invited, they are in control of everything and but don't feel left out if you are not, because they will be sure to post their triumph on social media and text you about it.

Exploitation of gift giving

As narcissists like to play games and have power trips, during the holidays they get to do both. For example, during a Christmas event with gift giving, the narcissist will not only show off their presents, they are telling others that their gifts are better or going to be better. If you happen to get a gift from the narcissist, instead of letting you enjoy it, you will suffer through the tremendous amount of effort they had to endure while getting that specific gift for you. They will somehow turn the gift giving situation onto themselves about how they should be thanked so much because of the effort they put in to get what they thought reminded them of you. Gift giving to the narcissist is not about anyone else but themselves.

The need for control

Ever witnessed or been a part of one child being more favored over the other or if there are no siblings then one person getting favored over everyone else? This is the narcissist's way to maintain control over a situation. When they favor one person, but single out another, they are asking to get criticized. This brings about conflict because in many cases you are actually at the narcissists house, so what comes next is "if you don't like it, get out."

The narcissistic mother (or father)

This doesn't necessarily have to happen just at holiday events, but as you have learned earlier in this chapter, there is always a 'scapegoat' of the family. In short, the one who calls it like it is. However, this scapegoat always gets the most trouble or abuse because of the way they are. All other children come to the defense of their narcissistic mother as an attempt not to become abused or belittled when they disagree with her version of the truth–called gas lighting. The scapegoat however, becomes the 'black sheep' and gets singled out by not just the mother, but the rest of the family as well as a result of the criticizing behavior from the 'goat.' While the scapegoat gets kicked out or singled out, everyone else goes about their ways of seeing and viewing things as the mother does because this is how they were raised. Remember this as the discard process of narcissistic abuse.

While holidays are supposed to be fun, they are almost always ruined when hosted by or invited in by a narcissist. The best way to deal with a holiday that involves narcissistic people is to enjoy the event, tolerate the individual, and once it's over avoid them for as long as you can while making better choices and a life for yourself. That said, can a narcissistic family change? As you have learned, yes, they can but it takes a great amount of effort and work. The cycle has to stop in order to break the influence of narcissism.

Chapter 5: Making Amends

Making amends with yourself is the first step to forgiving anyone else. But first you must understand what it means to forgive and make amends. When you forgive yourself, you can make wise decisions about whether you should forgive your abuser (the narcissist) and you can learn what a true apology means. The reason it is in your best interest to forgive yourself first before anything else is because along the abusive journey you endured, you might have dealt with friendships inappropriately, broken trust, or maybe you lost yourself along the way. Part of your own forgiveness is to let go of the baggage and anger you have built up through it all and release it so that you can live a fulfilling and successful life. Here are a few suggestions on how to forgive yourself when you feel at your worst and when shame takes over:

Be aware of your emotions

A lot of times, attempts at forgiving ourselves fail because we push away the emotions that we can't handle like guilt, anger, sadness, and shame. In order to truly forgive yourself for the burdens you have caused, you must take a moment and process each emotion individually. Accept the emotion, feel the emotion, and then let it go.

Recognize your apology

Uh oh! Did you make a mistake? Was it a big failure this time? Stop before you start spiraling down into a hole full of shame and guilt. What did you learn from this mistake? Paying attention and recognizing what you did wrong, and then talking back to your failures can help you take accountability for your actions. It may also help you to free yourself of the weight you hold on your shoulders or in your heart.

Think of your failures as personal growth

You cannot succeed without failure – you cannot fail without success. Every opportunity for growth is a learning curve, and we are not perfect. Let go of what the narcissist says and start to pay attention to how you really feel. So you made a big mistake, there is nothing you can do about it now. There is no greater amount of abuse you will endure than from yourself focusing on the mistake. Use what you have learned and move on by not doing it again.

Talk to your inner critic

Writing in a journal is perhaps the easiest way to talk back to your inner critic. Write down what your mind is telling you, and then write a response for it while looking at is as if a friend wrote you the letter. When you do this, you are teaching yourself how to identify your thought patterns and figuring out the root of your self-sabotage. Also, use this time to make a list of all the things you are proud of about yourself which can help boost your confidence when those dark days roll around.

Show self-love

Self-love is about knowing your weaknesses but focusing on your strengths. It's about learning how to accept yourself for who you are--unconditionally. So maybe you haven't had the best of luck at knowing how to love yourself based on your previous experiences. Don't let this bring you down and stop you from being who you are. Show yourself kindness and compassion, be patient with yourself and your emotions, and learn to reach out when you need help. All of these things are about loving yourself in ways that you won't need anyone else to do it for you.

Learning to forgive yourself is one thing, but do you really have to forgive the narcissist who put you in the frame of mind to have to forgive yourself? These previous suggestions work at any time you feel bad for something, but forgiveness also comes in the form of having to forgive others as well. However, the question still remains–do you really have to forgive the narcissist?

When thinking about this question, there are a few things to consider before making the choice to forgive (or to not forgive). All the scenarios depict what could happen if you seek forgiveness from the narcissist:

- They may try to exaggerate your mistake as something much larger than what you intended. Narcissists are sensitive to criticism. So in their opinion, they didn't do anything wrong, while you are the one to blame for something that you may have felt as harmless or minimal. The solution in this case—don't seek forgiveness from a narcissist and when accused, see the situation for what it is rather than letting them confuse you.

- Seeking forgiveness from a narcissist will result in them just gas lighting you and pointing more blame on you than actually admitting to their mistakes. They may accuse you of being overly sensitive and may make you feel bad for even asking them to apologize to begin with.

- A narcissist's view and perception of experiences may have you confused and can complicate the forgiveness process. For example, your narcissistic friends (or friends of the narcissist) may be upset with you for not forgiving the person for xxx reason. In this sense, you may develop their way of perceiving the situation, which causes self-doubt and a distortion to what is 'right' and 'wrong' in your mind and with your intuition.

Going back to the question – can I forgive the narcissist? Forgiveness means to seek justice or to have justice over something and have it handled effectively. Narcissists cannot help being narcissistic due to the disorder they suffer with (intentionally or unintentionally), so there really is no true justice. This suggests there is nothing to forgive or be forgiven for. Even though the person with NPD has a disorder, they still have choices to make in every situation ahead of them. It is ultimately up to them about what they choose to do, which is not in your hands or your responsibility. When anyone narcissistic or not makes the choice to not forgive or continue their behavior of making bad decisions, they aren't trying. Their apologies may seem repetitive and their actions get stuck in a continuous loop. Yes narcissists struggle with empathy and remorse for their actions, but does that mean you need to enable it? If you want to forgive them, start by forgiving yourself for suffering through the relationship before making the choice to forgive them. If you are going to forgive them for everything they have done, do it discreetly and to yourself otherwise conflict could arise.

Apologies

An apology is meant to be sincere and authentic. True apologies come from the heart with much thought behind them to make them unique and genuine. To be truly apologetic, someone must have empathy, the ability to sympathize, and have a clear level of emotional intelligence. If you have ever said sorry and meant it, you may have thought it through, and you knew that you were in the wrong. This is what it means to be able to take responsibility for your actions. To be accountable, means that you can fully admit to your mistakes, swallow your pride, and sincerely confess to your wrong doing. These traits – and what it takes to truly be apologetic are what the narcissist does not possess. Now that you have learned about forgiveness, and why it may or may not be a good idea to forgive the narcissist, let's take a closer look at what *fake* apologies are so we can see the difference between fake and genuine condolences.

"I am sorry if xxx." This type of apology only suggests that something *might* have happened not that they are truly sorry even if it didn't.

- *I am sorry IF I did something inappropriate.*

- *I am sorry IF I offended you.*

"I am sorry that you xxx." A blame game is what the narcissist will do, so this type of apology is their way of blaming you but trying to seem apologetic. This puts the focus of the apology on being solely your fault and no one else's even if it was their fault.

- *I am sorry THAT you are a sensitive person.*

- *I am sorry THAT you feel I did the wrong thing.*

- *I am sorry THAT I am a horrible person.*

"I am sorry but xxx." Anything that comes before a 'but' in a sentence or interaction means nothing because there is an excuse to get rid of everything said before the 'but.'

- *I am sorry, BUT you should be more aware of how you handle things.*

- *I am sorry, BUT everyone else didn't seem to mind.*

- *I am sorry, BUT at least I was honest with you.*

- *I am sorry, BUT I am not perfect.*

"I was just xxx." This isn't a real sorry because the person stating it is justifying their behavior. They are arguing your feelings for being hurt because their actions were justifiable or harmless.

- *I was JUST joking.*

- *I was JUST trying to relieve your tension.*

- *I was JUST trying to help you see from my perspective.*

- *I was JUST being the mediator.*

"You know I xxx." Talking someone out of the way they feel is like forcing responsibility on someone else because they are accountable for *your* actions and behaviors. It's the type of apology that states: "I have nothing to apologize for because you know I xxx."

- *You already know I am sorry —it's a given.*

- *You know I didn't mean it—stop being dramatic.*

- *You know I would never intentionally cause you pain—so get over it.*

"Xxx told me I should apologize." An apology like this one is the opposite of sincere, because the person actually had to be told to apologize. It means their ego means more to them than your feelings or their mistakes. It also shows that they never intended to apologize but they were told to, so now it's a half apology because of an obligation.

- *Our mutual friend said I should apologize because they said I hurt your feelings.*

- *Your mother asked me to apologize to you, so I am sorry.*

- *My partner made me realize how I made you feel and so I should apologize.*

A true apology from someone who shows sincerity and authenticity apologizes because they know they need to and because they know they made a mistake. Apologies do not come with conditions or obligations, they just happen because the person is sincerely upset about it as much as you are. It has to come from the heart when someone truly feels as though they don't want to lose the friendship; they show that they genuinely care about their mistake.

Building Healthy Relationships

Healthy relationships (friendships, spouses, coworkers, etc.) are the opposite of what it's like to live and be with a narcissist. It's when two people can come to an understanding and have a level of respect for each other that doesn't cross boundaries. This, in result, emphasizes the importance of trust, honesty, and support. A narcissist does not play fair, nor do they know how to communicate very well which is essential in growing, developing, and improving healthy and supportive alliances. If you have endured an unhealthy narcissistic relationship with a family member or otherwise, you may have been neglected and isolated, which might have caused you lose a few friends along the way. If this sounds familiar, follow the following tips in order to rebuild your relationships so that you can live a happier life full of supportive people around you.

1.Implement a polite and calm conversation

Before starting your conversation, you must prepare for what you are going to say. Start thinking about why your friendship ended in the first place. Think about the wrong you did and the role you played in your relationship falling apart. Only then should you go on to figure out what they did, because it is important they also know–after your apology, of course. If they have you blocked and you are unable to text them, use a friend's phone, or try to get to their house to leave them a letter in their mailbox. For this step, be brief: a quick hello, my name is xxx and I would like to talk about xxx please give me a call or reach out. A simple note no more than short, sweet, and straight to the point is all you need right now, because it's your turn to wait for their response.

2.Be 100% clear on what you want

Once they have reached back out to you, make sure that you are open, straightforward, and authentic about getting what you want out of the interaction. Is it to be friends again? Is it to be acquaintances while letting bygones be bygones? Whatever it is make sure you have thoroughly thought this through.

3.Be genuinely honest in a polite way

Throughout the conversation, the opposing party may have some needs they want to talk about as well. They will want to tell you their side of the story and how they feel. Make sure to listen effectively, pay attention to small details, and continue reading their body language for signs on *if* you should respond. During the interaction, make sure that you are neither offensive nor defensive. Keep in mind of what you are doing and feeling also; if it cannot be rehashed, then it may be best to accept this part, shut your mouth, and move forward. At least you tried.

4.Solve the problem

You should know by this moment in the conversation about their concerns, feelings, wants, and needs if you are going to try to rebuild. Work together to try to solve whatever the problem was to begin with. Make amends by showing how much you thought about your friendship and explain to them how you will do better. Also, ask for them to let you know what you can still continue to do as well.

5.Release perfectionism

Perfectionism is about wanting and maintaining complete control. Have control over yourself and what you feel, but never over another person or circumstance. Don't expect the conversation to end smoothly or go perfectly. Understand that they may reject your offer to rekindle your relationship. When interacting with them, remember to take a step back and pay attention to your emotions and how you want to react.

6.Give a sincere apology

We talked about forgiveness, and we talked about apologies. When you are apologizing, really concentrate on exactly it is that you are sorry for. Are you sorry that the relationship ended by doing xxx or because you acted inappropriately? Or are you sorry for not acting sooner than you should have? What have you learned in this mistake you made? Forgiveness is difficult for most people, but if you have forgiven yourself properly then whatever their response is, won't matter as you have already given yourself true forgiveness and all you can do is be better for yourself.

7.Be accountable

What exactly did you do? It's wise to name not only the things you did, but also name how you have hurt them and how you made them feel (preferably without them saying it). Don't expect anything from them in return through this process. Just explain to them what you are mainly responsible for. By doing this, you show authenticity and the potential or the want to do better.

8.Think *and be* positive

When you are stuck on negativity, you are going to get negativity. Before diving into the conversation at all, make sure you are in a good mood, and your thoughts about the outcome are set to auto-positive. When you go into the conversation with a positive attitude, it could change the whole dynamic of the interaction, which shows confidence and the opposing party will follow your lead.

9.Create healthy boundaries

While giving your apologies, and working with them to see how you can fix things and move forward, don't forget about your own personal morals. Think about what you stand for first and foremost. As much as you messed up, you wouldn't want to let your complete guard down because of the vulnerability you are putting yourself in. At some point, remember to remind them that you still stand for your own beliefs and wouldn't want those beliefs to be crossed either.

10.Shoot towards both your goals

Oftentimes when you are in the midst of a discussion, it seems to steer off topic, remember why you are here talking to your friend: to rebuild and improve your relationship. The object or the outcome of your interaction is to apologize while solving your problems and listening to their wants and needs while also keeping your boundaries in check. If the conversation is going well, feel free to invite them out with you another time and continue growing and strengthening your bond.

11.Learn how to say goodbye

In any encounter you endure, you may come across people who you just can't get along with or who were only meant to be in your life as a lesson or for a short period of time. Accept that you cannot perfect every relationship you have and be okay with having to say goodbye if that's what it comes down to. Besides, if the person is continuing to be negative or hostile, these are the people you are trying to stay away from in the first place and in the long run it might be for the best.

Rebuilding and putting a relationship back together is not just about one person (in this case you), it's about both individuals. It's about working towards a goal where you can both agree and learn to "agree to disagree." Healthy relationships are about communication, compromise, sacrifice, and commitment. If you have these fundamental ingredients in your supportive relationships, then a friendship, family relationship, or long-term partner (or whatever you seek out of it) will be most beneficial for both parties. On the other hand, if your relationship cannot be rekindled, then the learning experience of it is how you move on and move forward with your life while simultaneously ending this relationship chapter with healthy closure.

How to Say Goodbye to the Narcissist

By this point, you should know whether or not there is a narcissist in your life or in your family. By now, you should have also learned that trying to make any type of amends with the narcissist is most likely going to get you nowhere. It's hard to say goodbye to anyone, much less a family member, who has wronged you but the point is that everyone should show some sort of accountability for their actions. Everyone on this planet has choices they can make and narcissists--whether their disorder controls them or not–have options and decisions to choose from as well. Maybe you have come to your narcissistic mother or sibling and tried to explain to them the consequences of their actions; or maybe you have tried to reach out to them many times to *share* your success with them. The outcome always remains the same, doesn't it? The narcissist will either steal your spotlight by returning the conversation back to them, use you for something, or charm you out of your 'insensitivity' and 'criticism,' at least in their eyes. As hard as it may be to imagine life without them, take a second to really think about life without them. Imagine the freedom. Imagine the lack of control and power they will hold over you. Imagine the ability to make your own decisions, etc. Now, imagine a life all your own where you can do what you wish the 'right' way. Cutting ties with your family members who are narcissistic is more beneficial for you than it will be for them. Yes, they might miss you–but only because you are their victim and have been for years. Yes, they might try to win you back into their lives though hoovering, but how much energy are you willing to continue feeding into their behavior? The one thing to understand when leaving a narcissist is that they instinctively lack empathy. It's not that they mean to, but it is bred into their nature to be the way they are. Yes, they can change but again it takes dedication, patience, and hard work that won't be fixed in just a few short years.

What seems to be the biggest fear when leaving a narcissistic family member behind is that you actually have the freedom to make your own choices and stand on your own. For so long you may have depended on and served your narcissistic parent or grandparent, but the reality is that they will continue to tie you down and hold you accountable for everything that is not your responsibility. Your self-esteem will continue to decrease, your mental health will continue to plummet, and your cycle will only be more difficult to break in the future. In all honesty, you know how it feels to grow up in a narcissistic household; you know the pain and the victimizing feelings that come with being involved in the environment. When we have children and start our own families, a lot of the time we tend to repeat history by teaching our children based on what we have experienced. The cycle of narcissism will only grow if you don't escape now. Your time is now to get healthier and learn ways to overcome your imbedded patterns from childhood. It is time to seek the help you need through counseling and or social groups. That will help you set your mind for the future so you can live a long and fulfilling life with many close friendships.

When you feel the urge to reach out to contact your family member, think first. Why are you reaching out? Do you want to tell them what you learned? Do you want to share your experiences? Do you want to try to get them to seek help so that you don't have to stay away anymore? Remind yourself that despite all that you want to do and try to do, the narcissist will take no responsibility. Sure, they may say they will take action, but only to get you sucked back in again. Remind yourself of the abuse and the manipulation tactics that have your mental health collapsing and your cycles repeating. Say one thing: "*It is not up to me to help them realize the long-term effect of their behavior.*" Narcissists will waste your time (if you haven't noticed already) trying to justify their apologies by making excuses for their actions, actions that in the end don't change anyways. Another way to look at it is if you cut ties now, it may just be enough for them to get the help they need losing you (fingers crossed) and you can return to share your experiences apart later in life. As you grow and start standing up for yourself, and gaining mental strength while implementing personal growth, you may just find that working towards something feels better than manipulated to get what you want. It's time to own who you are, dream big, and make your own choices to shoot yourself forward in your life.

Learning to heal from the goodbye

Cutting ties with a narcissist is one thing, but actually following through is a completely different challenge. There will be times where you will want to reach out, and other times where you reminisce silently about the good times you experienced with them. You may even wonder if they think about you from time to time as you think about them. However, as a narcissist does not have empathy they don't necessarily have the ability to manage their emotions either, so missing you and thinking about you may not happen as often as you would hope. This should be enough to understand that you deserve better. Cutting ties is inevitable no matter what. You may choose to forgive, or you may choose to strive to fix the bond you share, but the fact of the matter is that eventually, you are going to want to spread your wings and break free from the suffocating grasp of the narcissist. Here are a few tips on how to heal and obtain closure from your relationship.

1. Write a closure letter

The letter to say goodbye should be mainly for you. It will help you process your emotions and get out whatever needs to be said without actually saying it to them. It helps in forgiving what happened and also builds your own self-respect. You can choose to send the letter, but it would be more beneficial to keep it to yourself since the narcissist will probably just see it as an open door for further offenses. The letter should be solely for your own purpose so you can gain acceptance and closure over the relationship.

2. Process your emotions

You may be feeling rejected, responsible, sad, lonely, angry, relieved, or all of the above in a cloud of confusion. To fully come to acceptance that your relationship is over, it is best to feel every emotion one at a time. Cry if you need to, get angry if you must, and sit alone to process for further growth. Some things you can do is put all your memories like pictures, objects, and a list of songs together in a box. Carefully go through each thing, and reminisce when you need to. When you are ready you can give it back to them or give it away. For now it might make you feel better to keep it so that you can pull it down and process your emotions while you remember your times together.

3.Plan a closure ritual

Every relationship, whether it's healthy or not, is symbolic. Creating a ceremony for forgiveness and the goodbyes can help you accept that your ties are cut off. Find something they gave you and shred it or donate it to release the negative energy. Or, if that's too difficult, find something that reminds you of them like a song or a poem and change the lyrics or verses into a closure setting. Releasing the negative energy you hold onto will help you get out of your slump and back into the game of personal improvement.

4.Fill the void

Usually when we have lost something, we feel empty and unsatisfied. We feel lonely and a little broken. The narcissist was your addiction and you must fill the void by replacing the negative addiction with something better. For example, if you just quit smoking you will need a new habit to take its place. Every time you have a nicotine craving you might choose to go for a run or be creative to distract yourself from wanting a cigarette. You can do the same with the void you feel from the narcissist. Be adaptable to change and look at this new experience as an opportunity to better your life.

5.Plan for your future

Oftentimes, the narcissist will reach out to you eventually. You may not be able to avoid running into them or seeing them through the holidays if they are family. However, making a plan for when these scenarios happen can really get you out of your comfort zone. Jot down quick reminders as to why you cut ties. Write down everything they did or how your relationship was unhealthy; Make a mental note about where you were heading with them in your life compared to where you are headed now. That way when you do run into them or have to talk to them, you can stand strong and have the courage to still walk away.

6.Be patient with the pain

The first step in letting go of the pain and the emptiness in your heart is to own your emotions and acknowledge them. Also acknowledge the fact that these feelings won't last forever. Understand that it is hard now, but as time goes by and with everything you are trying to do, it will get better and easier. Be patient with your feelings because when you try to avoid them, they will only get worse creating a louder inner critic in your mind. The inner critic is an unhelpful negative voice that reminds you of all your weaknesses. You just escaped a narcissist; you don't need your mind to be one too. So be patient and learn that it is okay to feel as you do in this moment.

7.Don't take anything personally

This step is perhaps the most important step of them all. Taking something personal means that you still carry the burdens of what the narcissist brought onto you. You must remember that their choices, actions, behaviors and lifestyle are not your responsibility. It never was. Their faults and weaknesses are and never were your challenges to take on. Let this weight release from your shoulders and remember that the way they live their lives and the opinions they hold have nothing to do with you. Taking it personally with this type of thinking puts the burden of responsibility onto yourself. How much abuse are you willing to take from yourself, never mind anyone else. Own who you are and never take what someone else says or does personally.

When it comes to saying goodbye to the one person who may have been there for you at one point, there are a few things to consider. Maybe you have been taught that through thick and thin, family should be there. Maybe you have been raised to never give up. But ask yourself: How much pain, hurt, and difficulty are you willing to take before you completely lose all control? Family does not necessarily mean blood, and blood doesn't have to be family. You deserve happiness. You deserve friendship. You deserve forgiveness and gratitude. You deserve to learn how to give this to yourself by obtaining freedom from the narcissistic relationship.

Chapter 6: Reclaim Your Life

Now that you have learned how to make amends with the people you care about, most importantly yourself, it's time to learn how to reclaim your life after narcissistic abuse. This part can be hard because if you were raised inside a narcissistic household then you have narcissistic traits engrained in your brain. Working to reclaim your life is not just about letting go of the narcissistic parent, grandparent, or sibling. It's about learning how to release the inner narcissist within yourself. There are four pillars to overcoming the internal and external abuse you have suffered through: self-esteem, self-worth, self-trust, and self-love.

Self-esteem

Imagine having complete control over your mind, body, and behaviors. No longer is there someone else brainwashing you to believe one thing, and manipulating you into doing another thing. Self-esteem is about noticing your perception of the world around you and what kind of effect you have on your environment. If you have constantly been sabotaging everything around you to the point of self-destruction then you do not have a high self-esteem level. Ultimately, a high self-esteem would be evident if you are confident in who you are as an individual without bowing down to the expectations or needs of others.

Self-esteem is mostly increased by the way you talk to yourself. If you are constantly listening to your inner-critic about all of the reason why you cannot do something, then you eventually start to believe it. You might find yourself trying to escape this negative self-talk by spending money on things you don't need or taking up an addictive substance like drinking alcohol and smoking cigarettes. This behavior shows that you aren't trying. While self-esteem is about how you carry yourself, your reputation amongst others at this point may not be the best either. This can also decrease levels of self-esteem and happiness even more. Self-esteem also decreases when you try and try at things, like fixing your narcissistic relationship, and no matter what you do or how hard you try, you just keep failing.

In order to build your self-esteem again, you must do things you are good at (like working or being creative) while also noticing your weaknesses (like building a narcissistic relationship). Addressing both of these aspects builds strength as well. Whether you have been raised in a narcissistic environment or you have met a narcissist who drew you into them, the reason your self-esteem may not be up to par is because you have taken all that you went through personally. As you should have learned by now, narcissistic abuse is not to be taken personally as it is their baggage and their faults that they have succeeded in projecting onto you. When rebuilding your self-esteem, ask yourself: What is something I can control right now in this moment? The answer should be easy enough, start taking better care of yourself that is something you can always control. So maybe you have become depressed, anxious or fallen into the early stages of PTSD. As a result, you may not feel like getting out of bed, getting dressed, or taking a shower and eating. All of these tasks are simple tasks you can start controlling right now.

The start of your self-esteem journey might be slow. You will not be gaining it back all at once but little by little as you continue doing small things that make you feel good and better about yourself every day. The more accomplished you feel, the more confidence you will have to tackle bigger tasks like turning that creative story into an outline or building the business plans you have been putting off for years. Remember to reward yourself with each accomplishment no matter how big or small. This will teach your brain that you are moving in the right direction, which will help in quieting that inner-critic who tells you that you can't do something.

Self-worth

Self-esteem, in short, is about being confident enough to be who you are with no expectations or bending to how others want you to be. However, self-worth takes self-esteem to the next level. It's about knowing what you stand for, holding true to your values, and respecting yourself enough to stand up for everything that makes you who you are. Of course a certain amount of confidence will get you to feel worthy, but ultimately self-worth is about accepting you for you and knowing what you're worth and what you deserve—which is not to be abused by a narcissist ever again.

If you feel an overload of guilt, shame, embarrassment of yourself, and unworthiness then you definitely have low levels of self-worth. This would make sense if you had been told your whole life that you are not good enough or how you are only good enough when you do excessively great things. You were taught to be a perfectionist and that failure is unacceptable. However, this thought process decreases your level of self-worth because if you are not 'perfect' then you aren't worthy enough to have what you want. The narcissist probably made you feel like you didn't have a voice or that you weren't free to say and do as you please in a respective manner. No, instead you were taught that failure is looked down upon, negative feelings were unacceptable, and if you weren't living to serve them a purpose then your worth meant nothing. A lifetime (up to this point) of this can have you second-guessing and compromising all the decisions you make when you finally do take a stand and decide to cut ties and go off on your own. Low levels of self-worth will keep you connected to the narcissist because they have implemented in your brain that you will never succeed in life without them.

Have you ever been told that you were a 'push-over'? That you are too empathetic or put many others in front of your own needs as a way to 'impress' or make yourself feel better? Lack of self-worth is when you struggle to stand up for yourself, it's when someone budges in front of you and you sit back quietly not saying anything. It's when you tell yourself how weak you are because you cannot say no. Then when you do say no, you beat yourself up because you fear the other person is now mad at you, and you can't handle that.

As long as you continue to feel worthless and incompetent, the narcissist will always have power over you. To develop and rebuild your self-worth is to start focusing on your courage and things you are grateful for. These things can be small like being grateful for waking up another day, or that you learned hard life lessons to get you seeing a different perspective. A lot of people don't know what a narcissist is and are lucky to leave if they figure out the signs and motives of their abuser. Be grateful that you are one individual that has now learned about them and is now learning how to overcome the abuse. Gaining courage means that you take risks to get further in your life than you are now. It's about working towards your goals every day and believing that you are just as important as everyone else. Start by taking small risks like speaking up at a family get-together or telling someone they need to stand in the back of the line. Apply for the job you want or go back to school. Taking risks is about finding your fears, and overcoming them little by little. When you do this whole-heartedly you build courage, which builds confidence, self-esteem, and self-worth.

Another way to build your self-worth is to really identify all your values and then be strict with them. Live by them and create boundaries so that they don't get crossed and you don't end up hurt again. Protect yourself by protecting your morals and believing in yourself to stand by what you want most in this world.

Self-trust

Ultimately self-trust is the ability to tune into your intuition (behind your inner-critic) and listening to that gut feeling within yourself that tells you to go for it or stay away. Self-trust is about believing in yourself and trusting that you know what is best for you.

The lack of self-trust revolves around feelings of self-doubt and fear. When you don't do something or avoid something based on your fears, you are strengthening self-doubt. Fear can either hold you back or push you forward, but mainly it can include anything and everything. You may fear taking risks or connecting with people. You may fear putting yourself out there or making decisions. Do you feel as though you are constantly second-guessing yourself? Maybe you feel like you know what to do but because of the lack of self-trust (and the narcissistic abuse) you overthink your decisions to the point where you back out? For example, someone cuts in front of you and due to the lack of self-worth you want to say something. Then just as you try to say something, you freeze; a knot forms in your stomach and you second-guess your next move to the point where you just don't say anything. The lack of self-trust can paralyze anyone in the sense where decisions often become a chore. These decisions can be anything between what to grab at the grocery store, where to eat for dinner, or even what to wear to your best friend's birthday party.

As if you didn't already have insecurities about most things, now it's even worse due to your lack of self-trust. Self-trust can be built by listening to your intuition. When you listen to your intuition, you regularly check in with yourself. *How am I feeling right now? What vibe does that person give me? What are my thoughts around that idea?* Notice how these thoughts aren't about second-guessing, but actually tuning into what you are thinking, feeling, and wanting. When you check in with yourself, make sure to listen to your first or second response–anything else will have you second-guessing and over-thinking, which perpetuates more self-trust issues. Once you have fully tuned into your instinctive nature, the next step is to take action. For example, if your body and mind tell you that the vibe you get from a specific person is off, it's best to take action by being cautious of them. The more times listening to your intuition proves you right, the more trust you will develop within yourself.

Self-love

This act of reclaiming your life after the narcissistic abuse is perhaps the most important self-growth technique you can learn. Self-love is about nurturing your inner-child and caring for yourself in ways that no one else can. When you learn to love yourself for all that you are, every other aspect (self-worth, self-trust, and self-esteem) falls into place naturally.

When you don't love yourself or take care of yourself (the inner child), you may have feelings of self-judgment and self-denial. These feelings stem from the narcissistic abuse, as one of their techniques was to distort your reality and sense of judgment and perception. The behaviors that stem from this are, people pleasing, always saying yes when you want to say no, and compromising your own needs for others. Do you constantly put yourself down? Feel like you aren't good enough or worthy enough or even smart enough? Do you honor your commitments to yourself? Or make promises often that you don't keep because you save your down time for someone else? This is what it feels like when you lack self-love. Your behaviors or habits may be that you don't eat when you are hungry (or you eat too much); you never drink enough water; you smoke more than you should; you drink alcohol often; and you never make time for yourself. Do you have too many things to do and not enough time to do them? Or do you find yourself getting stressed over little things because you forgot about them? Self-love and care is about not pushing yourself to achieve the impossible. Give yourself time to slow down and buy that book you have been waiting for, watch that movie you have been dying to see, or take longer in the bath than you normally would.

One thing to understand about making compromises for other people is that everything is a big deal when it comes to your personal growth. So maybe your friend asked you to go to the mall with her, but you had plans to have a bath, maybe nap, or get your hair done. Instead, you say no to yourself and yes to them for the fear of letting them down. It may not seem like a big deal, but it really is. When you compromise yourself, you compromise your integrity, health, peace of mind, sanity, and well-being. These things may not show up immediately, but overtime the lack of self-love can be critically damaging. So, what are some ways you can love yourself again?

Identify the things you dislike the most in your world. Figure out from those things what you can change and if not how you can look at them differently. For example, if you are in a narcissistic relationship, you can change this by leaving. If you hate the place your living in but are stuck in a yearlong lease, think about how you can see it differently. How many more months do you have left, and maybe you need those months so you can save for something better afterwards. Is it your health that you aren't happy with? Make commitments to go to the gym and eat healthier. If you can't change your shape because you are constantly focusing on your freckles or the fact that you have brown eyes when you want green, you need to work on self-acceptance. Self-acceptance comes with self-approval and confidence. If this is the case for you, there could be an underlying root of the problem. A lot of times when we struggle to accept our self-image, it's because we have been told our legs are too fat or our eyes are too wide. One thing to keep in mind is that no one defines your self-image but you. Confidence shows sexiness and self-worth gives you the respect you need to tackle your lack of self-acceptance.

How to Say No More Often

One of the main problems for people that lack confidence and self-esteem is that they don't know how to say no. As previously mentioned, they compromise their wants and needs for other people because of their internal fears. You may think that by saying no to people, they will respect you less and even disappear out of your life. Quite often the opposite of this fear happens. Not only will you have a new sense of respect for yourself, so will other people, because confidence and self-esteem are very attractive qualities in someone. When people see that you are trying to do better for yourself, they will respect your boundaries more and may actually follow suit. However, those people who actually do disappear or become super upset with you for you saying no will show you what they were in your life for to begin with. Normally people who are oversensitive about getting let down or rejected are those who have internal problems with themselves and it has nothing to do with you. Plus, part of reclaiming your life is about identifying these toxic people and staying away from them. So, technically learning to say no is a win for you no matter how you choose to look at it.

Perhaps you have preconceived notions surrounding the thought of saying no such as being disliked, fear of rejection, or seeming like you are careless or selfish. The important thing to take from this is that when you have these fears, you can mark yourself off the narcissism list. Narcissists don't have these fears, so the fact that you do says more about your character than most. However, saying no is an important step towards self-confidence and self-esteem. It's a way to build upon these so that you no longer fall for the narcissist's abusive tactics anymore. When someone asks you for a favor, instead of instinctively saying yes, take a minute to think about it first and consider the following steps:

- **Keep your responses clear and simple:** This process might make you feel as though you are being rude, but actually you don't have to be impolite at all when you say no. Simply start by thinking about your answer and if it's something you want to say no to say this: "Sorry but I have already made plans and I cannot help you this afternoon."Or, "I cannot commit to helping you right now as I have other things going on at the moment."These responses are short, sweet, and to the point.

- **Take time to think:** If someone comes to you and wants an answer now, you should never give in at that moment. Buy yourself some time by saying "Sorry, but I need some more time to think about it. I will get back to you." When you take extra time to think about your response, you will find yourself to be more confident with saying no later.

- **Compromise:** A compromise should only be if you truly want to help but only have a small time frame to do it. Let them know you have plans, but you are available within xxx times and come to a compromise on when you are going to help them.

- **Refusal and rejection are not the same things:** Refusal is about turning down a request; rejection is about turning away from a person. You are not turning down a person; you are turning down a request. So while you are saying no, make sure that you can make plans to get together another day when you actually do have time.

- **Be true to you:** Remember the talk about self-love and boundaries? Make sure that whenever you do say yes, it doesn't compromise your own morals and values. Be honest with yourself, do you want to do this or not?

The inability to say no promotes stress, exhaustion, and irritability. The ability to say no promotes inner peace, self-understanding, and respect. Don't spend hours obsessing over saying no, spend time evaluating yourself and your needs to grow and recover from the narcissistic abuse. Also, make time for family and supportive friends along with enjoying your down time for the sake of your sanity.

Creating Boundaries with Narcissists

The sole purpose and insight of a narcissist is to have full control, which by default doesn't set very strict boundaries for their own life. Due to their low self-esteem issues and an overload of insecurities, they resent or envy those who *do* set boundaries. In this case, they stay away from people who have solid values and strict inner confidence, because it would be a waste of their time to try to get into the confident individual's head. So, in order to reclaim your life and your sanity over the narcissist, it is most essential to set these boundaries as soon as possible as a protection barrier between you and those who abused you. So, how do you set boundaries with narcissists particularly? Here is how:

1.Know where the line is

Take a look at your values; they could be putting family first, not abusing animals, being a vegan or vegetarian, having respect, etc. While doing this, your focus should be on what you are willing to accept and what you are not. For example, you may not be willing to accept any type of control or negative influences. One way to be clear in your boundaries is letting the narcissist know that if they continue to blackmail, gas light, or control your actions, you will leave the conversation until they are willing to respect your values. If it continues, since you already said the first warning, you need to make it clear again, then walk away right after. That way you don't escalate the conflict and you will feel better about yourself for not engaging. Being clear about where the line is can leave you feeling confident, relaxed, and stronger.

2.Have an escape plan

Everyone has the freedom to protect their own rights. So, if you need to walk away or escape an unsafe situation. You do not need permission to leave. Just do it. At any given time, whether you need to make an excuse to leave or you need to have a supportive friend create an excuse for you, you have the ability to recognize disrespectful behavior and remove yourself from it. Another escape route may be that you set an alarm on your phone previous to the engagement, then use the alarm as an excuse to take the call—whether there is an actual call or not. This will stall the situation and give you some time to create a dialogue about how you need to leave—no explanation necessary.

3.There is no need for an explanation

Most times in a narcissistic interaction, you may get interrogated with a bunch of questions that are potentially none of their business. When they ask you things such as: "How do you spend your money? Where are you moving to? Why have you been so busy?" You can respond with: "That information is my business and I do not wish to share." Of course after that, they may call you out and make you feel guilty for not sharing with them, but the less they know the less they can hold over you later. When they continue to be rude–because they will–resort back to rule number one: where to draw the line.

4.Name their abuse tactic

Narcissists are not masters at knowing their emotions, thoughts, and actions as comes with the NPD; however, you can still remind them of what they are doing wrong. They may see it as the 'blame game;' but in actuality, you are creating solid grounds to not be abused. For example, when they say "you will get what you deserve" and based on how they have said that in the past you can respond with "I feel like that was a passive aggressive insult." Even if they deny it (because they will) you trust yourself enough to know what is happening in this moment. You can also let them know that you noticed them cutting you off every time you try to talk. Make them aware of their actions and give them the choice to stop. Otherwise resort again back to rule number one.

5.Re-center the focus to yourself

After they have interrupted and you, boldly make them aware. You can then return the focus back to what you were saying. Sometimes though, it is best to just walk away, because you know in your heart if they are listening effectively or merely listening just to respond and talk about themselves as is their habit. To avoid getting caught up in their social abuse or passive aggressive ways, check in with yourself to identify how you are feeling. When you notice your own moods, thoughts, and urges, you can defuse the situation by responding maturely to the interaction. If you do not check in with yourself, you may act upon your urge and engage in the narcissist's behavior, which only helps create more conflict, helping the narcissist win.

6.Prepare for having to do this more than once

Narcissistic people only think of themselves, so forget about you and the boundaries you have created originally. Maybe they haven't forgotten, but it's the fact that they just don't really care. Having to repeat your boundaries or remind them about your boundaries is going to be a process you need to take every time.

7.Remember self-love

Part of self-love is knowing when to walk away and knowing when you are being disrespected. The best way to stay on track with your self-love is to remind yourself of the years of control they had over you while growing up. Understand that if you give into their charm and persuasion, you will be living a life of constant abuse again. Yes, they can change, but they have to want to change first.

8. Focus on your inner growth

One of the most important steps to follow is to continuously try to focus on yourself and your personal growth. When a narcissist sees that you are working on yourself and will not stand for their abuse any longer, they will back down because they will feel incompetent towards you and resent your self-growth. A few things to ask yourself so that you stay on track are: *What do I stand for? Do I want to engage and feel small or incompetent? What would be the best resolution for myself right now?* Your obvious answers should be related to growing into the individual you have wanted to be and gaining a sense of self-respect. With this thought in mind, you can escape their reality and create a strong foundation for yourself.

9. Strong boundaries always end with consequences

Don't worry about letting them down or hurting their feelings. Narcissists, again, only think about themselves and their own struggles. They use these struggles to bring you down in your process. When you set good boundaries, be aware that your boundaries come with consequences to your and their actions. For example, when the narcissist chooses to project their feelings onto you, you can either walk away to defuse conflict or call them out and deal with it in the moment. Again, no explanation is needed. A narcissist is like an overgrown child, so in this sense you must act on your boundaries or they will take advantage of you the first chance they get.

Keep in mind that as you set these healthy boundaries for yourself, you are going to get negative responses from them as well. They may threaten you, gaslight you, spread gossip or rumors, or disown you. Pick your battles and do not engage into their negative and narcissistic behavior. Ask yourself what the price is that you will pay if you were to bow down to them again. Setting healthy boundaries creates much needed self-respect and confidence, which will result in them leaving you behind anyways. When you become aware of your own personal feelings you will understand the prices you are willing to pay. I assure you that price is less than what the narcissist will put you through (Neuharth, 2019).

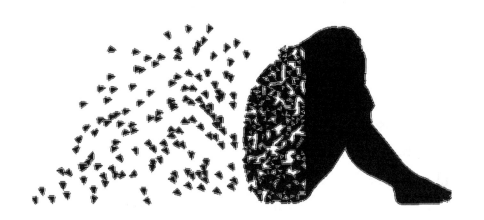

Conclusion

You now have learned about narcissism, what NPD is, how to define and spot a narcissist, along with the many disadvantages you have resulting from the abuse that a narcissist holds over you. The question about whether or not a narcissist can change has been answered. You now have enough information to start your journey to recovery and reclaim everything you have been searching for in your life. The most beneficial thing you can do for yourself, in escaping the narcissist, is to love yourself and present healthy, strict boundaries. From this moment on, you have the power to take your control back and to not let the narcissistic family members dictate what you do with your adult life.

It may be hard to let go of a family member that you have grown up with. But as mentioned, all you need to do in your weaker moments is ask yourself one question: "What is the risk I'm taking by welcoming them back into my life?" Are you really willing to take that risk? If you truly want growth and freedom from their wrath, all you need to do is try. Remind yourself of their behavior and even resort back to the journal you created to give yourself a different perspective and shed some more light on your decision. Stop second-guessing and do it all for you from here on out.

References

Helpguide.org. (n.d.). Narcissistic Personality Disorder. Retrieved from

https://www.helpguide.org/articles/mental-disorders/narcissistic-personality-disorder.htm
Mayo Clinic. (2017) Narcissistic Personality Disorder.) Retrieved from

https://www.mayoclinic.org/diseases-conditions/narcissistic-personality-disorder/symptoms-causes/syc-20366662
Heitler, S. (2012) Are You a Narcissist? 6 Sure Signs Of Narcissism. Retrieved from

https://www.psychologytoday.com/ca/blog/resolution-not-conflict/201210/are-you-narcissist-6-sure-signs-narcissism
Johnson, B. (2017). Childhood Roots of Narcissistic Personality Disorder Retrieved from

https://www.psychologytoday.com/ca/blog/warning-signs-parents/201701/childhood-roots-narcissistic-personality-disorder
Greenberg, E. (2017). How Do Children Become Narcissists? Retrieved from

https://www.psychologytoday.com/ca/blog/understanding-narcissism/201705/how-do-children-become-narcissists

PsychAlive. (2018). The Problem with Narcissistic Parents. Retrieved from

https://www.psychalive.org/the-problem-with-narcissistic-parents/

Evans, M.T. (2017). A Deeper Look at Idolise, Devalue, and Discard--The Three Phases of Narcissistic Abuse Part 1. Retrieved from

https://blog.melanietoniaevans.com/idolise-devalue-discard-the-3-phases-of-narcissistic-abuse-part-1/

Arabi, S. (2019). 20 Diversion Tactics Highly Manipulative Narcissists, Sociopaths, and Psychopaths Use to Silence You. Retrieved from

https://thoughtcatalog.com/shahida-arabi/2016/06/20-diversion-tactics-highly-manipulative-narcissists-sociopaths-and-psychopaths-use-to-silence-you/

Lombardo, E. (2016). 7 Underlying Truths A Psychologist Wants You To Know About Narcissistic Behavior. Retrieved from

https://www.mindbodygreen.com/0-27567/7-underlying-truths-a-psychologist-wants-you-to-know-about-narcissistic-behavior.html

Dodgson, L. (2018). 8 Things That Can Keep You Trapped in a Relationship with a Narcissist. Retrieved from https://www.insider.com/things-that-trap-you-in-relationship-with-narcissist-2018-12#healing-and-protecting-yourself-9

Sarkis,S.A. (2016). How to Leave a Narcissist for Good. Retrieved from

https://www.psychologytoday.com/us/blog/here-there-and-everywhere/201606/how-leave-narcissist-good

Milstead, K. (2019). What is Hoovering? 23 Narcissistic Hoovering Tactics to Watch Out For. Retrieved from

https://fairytaleshadows.com/narcissist-hoovering-techniques/

Borresen, K. (2018). Can Narcissists Actually Change Their Ways? We Asked The Experts. Retrieved from

https://www.huffingtonpost.ca/entry/can-narcissist-change-their-ways_n_5a95a5fae4b03a8f3a23288c

Goodtherapy. (2018). How to Deal with a Narcissist. Retrieved from

https://www.goodtherapy.org/learn-about-therapy/issues/narcissism/how-to-deal

Palmatier, T.J. (2018). The First Holiday Season Without the Narcissist or Borderline. Retrieved from

http://shrink4men.com/2018/11/22/the-first-holiday-season-without-the-narcissist-or-borderline/

Streep, P. (2017). The Narcissistic Parent's Holiday Playbook. Retrieved from https://blogs.psychcentral.com/knotted/2017/11/the-narcissistic-parents-holiday-playbook-and-how-to-deal-with-it/

Healthline. (n.d.). 12 Tips for Forgiving Yourself. Retrieved from

https://www.healthline.com/health/how-to-forgive-yourself#1

Enright, R. (2018). Narcissism and Forgiveness: 4 Considerations for You. Retrieved from

https://www.healthline.com/health/how-to-forgive-yourself#1

Neuharth, D. (2019). The Top 12 Fake Apologies – And What Makes For An Authentic Apology. Retrieved from

https://blogs.psychcentral.com/love-matters/2018/06/the-top-12-fake-apologies-and-what-makes-for-an-authentic-apology/

Lifehack. (2014). 15 Ways to Build a Broken Relationship. Retrieved from

https://www.lifehack.org/articles/communication/15-ways-rebuild-broken-relationship.html

Boggs, A. (2017). Saying Goodbye To The Narcissist in Your Life. Retrieved from

https://www.theodysseyonline.com/saying-goodbye-to-the-narcissist-in-your-life

Borchard, T.J. (2018). 8 Steps to Closure When a Friendship Ends. Retrieved from https://psychcentral.com/blog/8-steps-to-closure-when-a-friendship-ends/

Medium. (2018). Pillars for Recovery After Narcissistic Abuse. Retrieved from

https://medium.com/@OwnYourReality/4-pillars-for-recovery-after-narcissistic-abuse-7195a40f0b6a

Collingwood, J. (2018). Learning To Say No. Retrieved from

https://psychcentral.com/lib/learning-to-say-no/

Neuharth, D. (2019). 11 Ways to Set Boundaries with Narcissists. Retrieved from

https://blogs.psychcentral.com/narcissism-decoded/2017/06/11-ways-to-set-boundaries-with-narcissists/

CPSIA information can be obtained
at www.ICGtesting.com
Printed in the USA
LVHW052303090723
751969LV00008B/593